D0810699

The
STRANGER
In Your
Bed

The
STRANGER
In Your
Bed

Dr. Rosalie Reichman

WILEY

JOHN WILEY & SONS
New York • Chichester • Brisbane • Toronto • Singapore

Portions of Chapter 12 are based on "7 Myths about Marriage,"
Bride's Magazine, August-September 1987.

Extract on page 170 is from Erich Fromm, *The Art of Loving*, ©
1956 by Harper & Row; Bantam edition published in 1963 by
arrangement with Harper & Row; page 17.

This publication is designed to provide accurate and
authoritative information in regard to the subject
matter covered. It is sold with the understanding that
the publisher is not engaged in rendering legal, accounting,
or other professional service. If legal advice or other
expert assistance is required, the services of a competent
professional person should be sought. *From a Declaration
of Principles jointly adopted by a Committee of the
American Bar Association and a Committee of Publishers.*

Library of Congress Cataloging-in-Publication Data

Reichman, Rosalie.
  The stranger in your bed.

  Bibliography: p.
  1. Intimacy (Psychology) I. Title.
BF575.I5R45   1989   158'.2   88-17379
ISBN 0-471-61124-7

Printed in the United States of America

10 9 8 7 6 5 4 3 2 1

For Joe, Carrie, Lisa, and Eric

Preface

As a clinical psychologist working with individuals and couples for about 18 years, I have seen hundreds of people who are lonely. Some are single and some are married, but most are looking for more in their relationships—more closeness, more understanding, more acceptance.

As I have led many of these people toward more realistic choices of mates and toward improvement in their current relationships, I have noticed many subtle but important characteristics of their relating. While some of them were obviously avoiding intimacy, most were erecting more indirect and hard-to-see barriers between themselves and others. I called these barriers "veils." Some people actively sought closeness but sabotaged it when they achieved it. They, too, placed veils between themselves and others.

I wrote this book for people such as these; I call them Intimacy Avoiders. It is designed for single people of both sexes who are looking for mates and want to understand their own ways of relating. They might see themselves and their potential mates in these descriptions. I also wrote this book for those already involved or married. Many of them are unhappy with their relationships and don't know why. What they read here will help them understand why and show them what to do about their problems.

In this book I delineate several different types of Intimacy Avoiders. I describe their behavior and give examples from my practice so that you can recognize aspects of them in yourself or your partner. I explain the reasons these people need to avoid closeness. Intimacy Avoiders fit into three major categories: Distancers, Pseudo-Intimates, and Intimacy Saboteurs. Although sharing some characteristics, these groups are basically different in the degree to which they avoid intimacy and in the reasons that propel them.

Distancers either actively avoid relationships or place very obvious barriers between themselves and their mates. Pseudo-Intimates appear to be closely involved but nonetheless avoid real intimacy by indirect means. Intimacy Saboteurs drive others away from them in subtle or not so subtle ways because of their behavior.

Although many books have been written about how to achieve greater intimacy and about people who avoid intimacy, most of them focus on one major type. Readers have no choice but to try to place their mates or themselves into the type a particular book describes. Since people are made up of many elements, they can often find something with which to identify, but this might give them an incomplete and therefore inaccurate picture of their particular problem. In this book I have attempted to overcome this difficulty by presenting several different types of Intimacy Avoider. While it certainly doesn't exhaust every possibility, it does cover the most common varieties. It is important to realize, however, that most people can't be fit into one type exactly. They may share characteristics with two or more types, and their behavior may have several causes.

Other books, whether written by men or women, also tend to portray women as victims. Women are seen either as unable to choose men wisely or as being willing to put up with anything for love. They are not given enough credit for being in charge of their own lives—for being responsible for their own ways of interacting with others. If men are presented as the sole problem, women will feel helpless and unable to change their relationships.

I don't see most women as victims, nor do I see most men as either abusive or avoidant. There are many people of both sexes who are victims, abusers, or avoiders. But the majority of men and women are trying their best to have a close relationship in spite of their fears and insecurities.

I have found that the old stereotype of men distancing from women while women approach men is not always true. I have seen many women who were Intimacy Avoiders and many men who wanted true intimacy. However, women, needing relationships and marriages—through which they have traditionally defined themselves—usually hide their own avoidant tendencies. They blame any lack of closeness in their relationships on their men.

I have also seen men who sabotaged intimacy because of their overdependency and neediness. That such men exist has often been overlooked because men usually disguise their neediness out of shame.

These apparent reversals of roles will probably be seen more frequently as women learn to define themselves more through their work and men become more open about their feelings.

In my descriptions of Intimacy Avoiders, I have often referred to them as either "he" or "she." This doesn't mean that certain types are confined to one or the other sex. Some are more common among either men or women, but frequently the gender I chose in my description was the same as the particular example I used. The examples come from my work with patients. However, some cases are presented as composites, and the identifying information has been changed to protect their confidentiality.

Use this book as a guide. It will lead you through the steps of recognizing your or your partner's problems, understanding them, and dealing with them. I have included concrete techniques for overcoming specific problems and achieving greater intimacy, which I have developed over the years and have found to be very effective with my clients.

While most of you will be able to use these suggestions to improve your relationships, some of you will need more. Although this book isn't meant to be a guide to therapy, I would be negligent in not mentioning that sometimes therapy is indicated. In the last chapter of the book, I have included some information about professional help—if you can't do it alone.

ROSALIE REICHMAN

Roslyn Estates, New York
December, 1988

Acknowledgments

First of all, I would like to thank my patients, who inspired me to write this book. By sharing with me the intimate details of their lives, as well as their innermost fears and desires, these men and women enabled me to better understand relationships and how they can go astray. Through their successful efforts to improve their own relationships, they also showed me how people can overcome barriers to intimacy.

My editor, Herb Reich, senior editor at John Wiley and Sons, Inc., deserves special thanks. His confidence in the book and his reassuring manner during its development provided the proper balance to my perfectionism. His judicious editing and suggestions were invaluable in improving the book.

I would also like to thank my husband, Joe, who read most of the book—more than once—and who offered many helpful and relevant comments. His support and inspiration from the book's inception have been very important to me.

My daughters, Carrie and Lisa, also warrant particular mention. They read sections of the book, offered their own unique viewpoints, and gave me much encouragement when I needed it.

My mother and father, although not directly involved in the book's production, also deserve thanks. They taught me about intimacy firsthand and demonstrated an intimate relationship at work throughout their marriage of 56 years. In addition, through their consistent encouragement of my education and achievement, they have made this book possible.

R.R.

Contents

1

What Is Your InQ?

"**I** just can't understand it. I wanted him so much, but now that he's asked me to marry him—I can't do it. I'm so afraid of ending up with a stranger in my bed," said Carol, tears forming in her eyes.

Carol is 28, but looks 20. She has striking green eyes and black hair. She's a strong-minded woman who always felt that she knew what she wanted. When she began dating Joe, she was very sure of her feelings for him. He had everything she ever wanted in a man—he was good-looking, charming and outgoing, and successful as an attorney. She began therapy because of nagging doubts she couldn't understand. She felt there was something wrong with the relationship, but she couldn't put her finger on what it was. She explained, "He's good to me, we get along well, and our sex life is great. Still—I don't know why, but I feel closer to my girlfriends. Maybe I'm expecting too much."

When we explored the situation further, we saw that Carol and Joe spent very little time alone together. All of their socializing revolved around his clients and their friends. When they did spend an evening alone together, he would nod off in front of the TV. They didn't talk very much, and when they did it was usually about their work. He never seemed interested in her feelings. No wonder she worried that she might wake up one day feeling that she had a stranger in her bed.

Many people whom I have seen, both in and out of therapy, feel that their lovers or spouses are strangers. Their relationships may appear perfect to everyone else, but they still feel lonely and alienated. Their complaints often center on problems with in-laws, money, or children, but they convey the underlying feeling of a lack of intimacy—a lack of warmth, of closeness, and of open sharing of thoughts and feelings.

Joan says, "My boyfriend says that he wants to get married but he can't leave his elderly mother."

"My girlfriend keeps putting off living together because we haven't saved enough money," says Ben.

"My husband seems to be devoted to me and the children, but he spends most of his time at the office or on the golf course," says Shelly.

Jerry says, "I feel lonely a good deal of the time because my wife is so involved with the children and her parents."

Are these people expecting too much? No! They, like Carol, and like you and me, want and need intimacy. However, they are unwittingly involved with Intimacy Avoiders (IAs).

Intimacy Avoiders are the strangers in your bed. They are trying to get close enough to be warm but are afraid of getting too close and being hurt. While believing they are seeking intimacy, IAs are engaged in a desperate attempt to avoid too much of it.

In spite of their outward appearances, many people are IAs. They may be searching for a relationship or already in one. Not knowing what real intimacy is, they are often unaware of avoiding it. They may desperately want closeness to others and not realize that they themselves are preventing it.

Intimacy Avoiders frequently believe they are comfortable with intimacy because they enjoy relationships with friends and casual dates or lovers. When more serious or closer relationships are unsuccessful, they blame it on the other person. If they have several relationships that fail and they are more psychologically sophisticated, they may blame it on their repeated choice of the wrong type of person. Intimacy Avoiders who are married or involved believe that their relationships are close and intimate. They do not recognize that they may be distancing by being too involved in work, their children, or other activities or people. They do not recognize that their constant fighting or difficulties with sex or money are part of their need to distance. While pretending to be involved with someone because they live with them, they, too, avoid real intimacy.

If you are involved with an IA (or are an IA yourself), you may be dissatisfied with your relationship and not understand why. You may not recognize that what you lack is true intimacy.

We all need intimacy. The only way to avoid loneliness is through this special closeness with another person. Most of us seek attachment with others at any cost—even when we become distressed in the process. For some, the quest seems futile and never ending—they continually choose the "wrong people." Some never marry or get involved, finding it impossible to find the right mate. We look at them with either pity or scorn, depending on whether we see them as forlorn or self-involved. But they are not the norm. Most of us form more or less lasting relationships with another person. Some of us marry or get involved only to separate. Yet even then, we usually try again, and again, hoping and believing that finding a new partner will be the answer to our problems.

Is marriage the answer? It certainly can be very gratifying. Some people remain married to the same person all their lives, having children and grandchildren with them. Yet even then they may feel lonely and isolated—experiencing an awful, unending, unbearable ache, not understanding why their efforts always seems to fail. The sad fact is that many married people are unhappy; and there is nothing more lonely than feeling alone when you are with someone you love.

Many think that good sex life is the answer. The popular media would have us believe that sex is the path to happiness. People have thus become very involved in learning new and better techniques leading to greater sexual satisfaction, increased sexual desire, and finding a good sex partner. However, my experience indicates that sex is not the primary problem of couples, and that more and better sex is not the solution. Sexual difficulties of all kinds are almost always symptoms of deeper problems in the relationship.

Then what is the answer? Recent research reveals that the most important ingredient in a happy marriage is the ability to talk over problems. According to some studies, happily married couples often seem to share a secret language. This communication is more important to marital satisfaction than frequency of sexual intercourse or how much in love the partners were before marriage. Compatibility of interests or personality also does not seem to be as vital as the ability to talk to each other.

In my work with people who are unhappy in their relationships, I find myself suggesting this more than anything else—that they talk to their partners, tell them how they feel. This sounds simple and almost too obvious, and while it is excellent advice, it is usually about as helpful as telling a hard driving person to "slow down" or an overanxious worrier to "stop worrying." Most people already know that communicating is desirable. Doing it is another matter.

All too frequently, people in troubled relationships have great difficulty expressing their deep feelings and thoughts. They fear that they won't make themselves understood and that their partners will either get angry with them or ignore them. Why can some people talk to each other and work out problems while others find it almost impossible?

The ability to communicate—to really talk to each other and hear each other about important matters—requires a closeness and an emotional openness between the partners. Couples have difficulty achieving this openness either because they lack the right methods or because they have emotional blocks. Usually I do not find these problems to be caused by lack of knowledge of what you "should" do. We are barraged by books and articles telling us the "rules" for better communicating, better loving, and better relating. Why can't we learn these "rules" and improve our relationships? Trying to follow such advice can lead to much frustration; it sounds so reasonable and yet can be so hard to do. What is too often ignored is that, in close relationships, people's reactions are not determined by logic or will, but by emotions and needs. IAs' emotions and needs—their fears, their insecurities—can be so strong that they prevent the IA from getting close to others.

What could be so threatening to Intimacy Avoiders that it might cause them to sabotage the closeness that they want so much? Intimacy is a risk! They must open up and give to another with no guarantee that what they give will be returned. To some extent, we are all afraid to take a risk with such high stakes. But IAs are more reluctant than others. Their underlying, often unconscious, feelings serve as veils between them and others. Some of these veils are fears, others are unreasonable "needs," and still others are unrealistic expectations. All of them can prevent people from getting what they want from relationships.

This book is about these Intimacy Avoiders and their veils. These veils come in many thicknesses and can have many layers. Some are opaque; others are more transparent.

I have formulated three basic types of Intimacy Avoiders: Distancers, Pseudo-Intimates, and Intimacy Saboteurs. The three types have some similarities, but they vary in the degree of the methods they use to prevent intimacy.

• Distancers tend to either actively avoid relationships or, while in relationships, to remain overly invested in themselves, their outside interests, or other people.

• Pseudo-Intimates are less obvious. They are usually involved in relationships and appear to the world to be close to their partners. They avoid real intimacy, however, by subtle means.

• Intimacy Saboteurs want to be close to others. But they cause others to distance from them because of their neediness, their excessive giving or controlling, or their other behaviors.

In the first section of this book, I will describe the most common types of Distancers, Pseudo-Intimates, and Intimacy Saboteurs, giving you examples of each from my therapy practice. I will explain how they act, and how their behavior creates obstacles to closeness.

The second section will help you understand why IAs behave as they do. Some of my explanations focus on fears while others deal with overdependency, low self-esteem, and difficulties with identity.

Most of the people described in the book finally overcame their problems. You can see what they did to achieve greater intimacy. The third section of the book will focus on how to deal with problems of intimacy avoidance. I will present specific techniques to help in conquering fears, overdependence, and other problems. I will also point out instances where it would be better to switch than fight.

By looking beneath the surface of your behavior and that of your partner, you can identify and better understand the particular fears and insecurities that stand in the way of your intimacy. Then you can work on achieving greater closeness in your relationships by following the step-by-step procedures for overcoming these barriers.

WHAT IS YOUR INTIMACY QUOTIENT (InQ)?

Is there enough intimacy in your current relationship? Are you an Intimacy Avoider? Is your partner or the person you're involved with? The questionnaire below could alert you to these possibilities and help you to assess your level of intimacy—your Intimacy Quotient (InQ). Take this quiz on some common signs of difficulties with relationship intimacy. For each question, mark *A* for frequently, *B* for sometimes, or *C* for rarely or never. A high score can mean that you, or your mate, or both of you are Intimacy Avoiders.

	A	*B*	*C*
1. It is difficult for me to refuse to do what my mate asks of me.	—	—	—
2. I find a great deal wrong with my mate.	—	—	—
3. I feel as if I have no "space" in my relationship.	—	—	—
4. I feel that I have the upper hand in my relationship.	—	—	—
5. My partner tries to tell me what to do too much.	—	—	—
6. I feel put down by my mate.	—	—	—
7. My mate is not available enough emotionally.	—	—	—
8. I am very sensitive to criticism from my mate.	—	—	—
9. I have difficulty asserting myself or making my needs clear to my partner.	—	—	—

10. I feel powerless in decision making with my mate. — — —

11. I feel that my partner has the upper hand in the relationship. — — —

12. I feel that I "have to" do what my partner asks. — — —

13. I feel jealous of my mate's other relationships. — — —

14. I worry about losing myself in my relationship. — — —

15. I feel trapped in my relationship. — — —

16. I feel controlled by my mate. — — —

17. I often wonder if I can "count on" my partner in an emergency. — — —

18. I feel angry at my partner's demands. — — —

19. I find myself spending more and more time at work or other activities. — — —

20. My partner finds a great deal of fault with me. — — —

21. I don't feel that my partner accepts me for what I am. — — —

22. I feel misunderstood by my mate. — — —

23. I find myself angry without knowing why. — — —

24. After spending time with my partner alone, I begin to feel bored. — — —

25. I feel taken advantage of. — — —

26. I am periodically turned off sexually. — — —

27. I feel insecure about my mate's love. — — —

28. My mate expects too much of me. — — —

29. When home alone with my mate, I find myself withdrawing into my own world—TV or work around the house. — — —

30. I wonder whether I made the wrong choice in a mate. — — —

31. I find myself "walking on eggs" with my mate. — — —

32. I worry that my mate will eventually leave me. — — —

33. I find myself daydreaming about someone else. — — —

34. I easily feel left out of situations with my partner and his friends or family. — — —

35. When I feel unfairly treated by my mate I get depressed and withdraw. — — —

Now score your test. Count 5 points for each A response, 3 points for each B, and 1 point for each C.

If you scored:

49 or under	You have no problems with intimacy, or your answers are not entirely truthful.
50–64	There are some difficulties in your relationships that should not be hard to overcome.
65–79	At least one of you is a strong intimacy avoider.
80 or over	There are very serious problems with intimacy in your relationship.

Intimacy Avoiders
The Strangers

2

Distancers

Distancers are the easiest IAs to spot. They are unmistakable avoiders of closeness. The veils they place between themselves and others are opaque and many-layered.

How do we know if we or our partners are distancers? Obviously, if someone continually dates different people and never gets involved with any of them, he is avoiding intimacy. No matter how much he blames his "bad luck in meeting people" or says, "All the good ones are married and what's left are the losers," and so on, we realize that he is afraid to get involved.

However, most distancers are more artful than that. Many of them do get involved, but always seem to find justification for never making a total commitment. They can get closer than those who never go beyond dating, but they lack the ability to take the final risk. These people are usually very good at coming up with new excuses for each failed relationship. Some of them are also quite adept at getting others to initiate the breakup so that it appears to all the world, including them, that they wanted more but were "dumped."

How can you tell the difference between those who are merely being selective and those who are avoiding intimacy? Examine their patterns of involvement. What are their reasons for breaking off each relationship? If after years of dating and many aborted involvements, they still cannot find anyone who is right for them, it is likely that they are distancers. Some of the most common types are described here. See if you can recognize your or your partner's patterns in the descriptions of the following characters.

THE PERFECTIONIST

Perfectionists have an exaggerated fear of making the wrong choice. Appearing merely to be too choosy—as if no one is good enough for them—they form short-term relationships but are unwilling to allow themselves to get attached to anyone. They say, "I don't want to close off other possibilities." They dread being "stuck" with someone who will not meet their needs or who will be boring or not be good enough in some other way. When they begin to care for someone, they suddenly feel trapped, and by too carefully scrutinizing their lover, they invariably find some "fatal flaw" to justify breaking off the relationship. For example, a Perfectionist might decide that his lover is too dependent or too involved with herself. Another time he might see her as too plain or not bright enough. No matter what her assets, when she gets too close he focuses on her faults. This super-discriminating stance, a perfect ploy for Perfectionists, prevents them from having to look at their own reluctance to get involved.

Why are they so unwilling to make a choice?

Sometimes Perfectionists are overly selective because they are protecting themselves from their own neediness. They are afraid their overwhelming need for closeness will overshadow their judgement, forcing them to make a precipitous and unfortunate commitment. Feeling so needy, they want their mates to be all-giving, to guarantee that their own needs will be met. Committing to one person, especially an imperfect one, and having to worry about meeting this person's needs as well as their own, is very frightening to them.

Another reason it is difficult for Perfectionists to allow themselves to get too close is their fear of rejection and humiliation. They have an impossibly high level of expectation for themselves as well as for their lovers. Secretly fearing that they can't live up to these expectations, they worry that close partners will see their imperfections and not want them or will belittle them. As a result, they often reject their lovers before their lovers can reject them. Since they feel so imperfect themselves, Perfectionists want their partners to enhance their image. They view them as reflections of their own worth, so their partners have to be perfect. Male Perfectionists never seem to find women beautiful and talented enough, while female Perfectionists can't find men who are rich and successful enough. Any discernible flaw in their lovers makes them feel belittled by association. They feel that having to accept an imperfect mate implies that they themselves aren't good enough. One woman questioned, "Am I so unlovable that I have to settle for him?"

Some Perfectionists' difficulties in selecting mates disguise fears of being controlled or manipulated. As soon as others get close enough to be important, these Distancers fear being taken over by them. On some level, they believe that loving and needing people means not being able to refuse their demands. Those who have this problem are usually subject to guilt or extreme fears of rejection. As a result, they feel compelled to comply with beloveds' requests, no matter how unreasonable or costly.

How do they develop these fears? Some Perfectionists were expected to be perfect when they were children and they may have felt that they couldn't live up to their parents' expectations. Often, they were expected to "make mommy happy" or "not upset mommy." As adults, it is impossible for them to have a close relationship and not feel the pressure of having to please their loved ones. As a result, Perfectionists feel being close to another person means leaving themselves open to becoming compliant and chronically angry and resentful.

Just such a problem is demonstrated by Mel, a young attorney. Successful in his law practice, attractive, and sought after by many women, Mel had been in many relationships. Every time, he exclaimed, "This time it's different: I'm in love." Yet with each relationship, before it became too serious, Mel found another excuse—"Susan is still officially married," "Iris has difficulty having orgasms," "Betsy wants too much from me and makes me feel guilty." In each case he suddenly became more attracted to other women and no longer felt turned on sexually by his current love.

He would often separate from the woman temporarily for a cooling-off period, so that he could reduce the intensity of the relationship to a more comfortable level. In spite of his behavior, he maintained he was looking for marriage but had not yet found the right woman.

In therapy, Mel began to realize that he was actively avoiding commitment. He saw that he became uncomfortable and felt threatened whenever anyone got too familiar. After some exploration, he was able to recognize that he was really afraid of being controlled. His mother had been a very demanding woman, getting him to do what she wanted by making him feel guilty. When a woman became important to him, he became frightened she would extract the pound of flesh that his mother had extracted from him. He feared that women didn't love him for himself, but only wanted him to fulfill their own needs. As a result, he was reluctant to give to them. When they were disappointed or angry, he felt guilty, as he had with his mother. So he would run away from them, blaming them for being unreasonable.

Mel acknowledged that his fear of being controlled was interfering with his desire for intimacy. He recognized that in order to realize his dream of a good marriage, he would have to work on his fears.

Sometimes the Perfectionist ploy is used by career women. They say they are looking for a permanent mate but in reality are petrified at the thought of marriage. In order to hide these fears from themselves, they blame the "lack of good men around" and find something wrong with each man they date.

Women who have spent a great deal of time and effort building a successful career may feel they have a lot to lose in marriage. They fear being subjugated to men. Often these women have grown up in households where the father was the controlling force while the mother spent her time and energy caring for the family. These women saw their mothers sacrifice their own personal and professional development for marriage, and they don't want to repeat this pattern in their own lives.

Although wanting closeness, women such as these are very much conflicted. They see marriage and children as a serious threat to their own growth and lifestyle. Some men are threatened by successful career women; these women assume *all* men are threatened. Some men will not make adjustments for their wives' professions; these women fear none of them will.

THE ROMANTICIST

The Romanticist is forever seeking the perfect romance. He usually falls in love, in an overidealized way, with a woman he hardly knows. From a distance, this woman seems perfect and wonderful. He might daydream about her and write love letters or poetry to her. Some Romanticists never go beyond this adolescent crush phase. They are afraid to approach their beloved, content to worship her from afar.

Many Romanticists do pursue their beloveds, attentive to romantic details—candlelit dinners, flowers, and gifts. If the objects of their desire respond but remain mysterious, cool, and distant, they will continue to be intrigued. They thrive on the romance and excitement of being "in love." However, they are in love with their fantasized image of the women, not the women themselves. They enjoy the intensity and insecurity of the chase. If they feel they are winning—attaining their goal—they quickly lose interest.

Sometimes Romanticists marry and spend their lives pursuing the affections of their spouses, whom they see as cold and withholding. They may appear, to all the world, as adoring, romantic spouses who are constantly wooing their mates.

If the Romanticist's love interest responds to him, he quickly becomes bored with her, and he becomes critical, like the Perfectionist. But unlike the Perfectionist, he will idealize and adore her as long as she is distant and aloof.

Why are Romanticists attracted to "hard-to-get" people? Frequently their mothers were detached and unresponsive. Because their mothers were their first loves, when they were young and impressionable, others who remind Romanticists of mother revive warm, loving feelings from childhood. They learned from these early experiences to expect to be treated coldly and to have to actively pursue love from others. Anyone who gives love freely to them is suspect.

Romanticists generally devalue anyone who cares for them. They have an underlying feeling of inferiority and fully believe that anyone who would accept them can't be very worthwhile. Only those who either reject them or keep them guessing are considered worthy of their love. If someone they love offers them affection, they react with distrust and fear. Since Romanticists are firmly convinced that no one could possibly love them, they immediately assume that affection from others is covering up ulterior motives. They tend to interpret the affection as teasing, deliberate provocation, or an attempt to humiliate them, so in order to protect themselves, Romanticists invariably reject such demonstrative suitors.

George is a 40-year-old engineer at a large aerospace corporation. He is known as a perpetual bachelor who is always bragging about the new woman he is seeing.

George says he wants to settle down and raise a family. His friends have tried to set him up with eligible women, but he usually finds them boring. The women he likes tend to be very involved with themselves or their careers. He says he likes their independence. Although he actively pursues them, they never seem to return his ardor. His friends tease him that he wants only what he can't have.

George's latest passion is Lisa, a stunningly beautiful model. He adores her and showers her with gifts. Although he says that his greatest wish is for her to love him, it seems clear to others that he will continue his pursuit only as long as she doesn't respond to him.

Why doesn't he choose women who are more receptive to him? What makes these distant women so appealing?

George's mother was quite restrained emotionally. He loved her and spent a great deal of time and energy during his childhood trying to win her over. She always appeared to him to be desirable in her aloof, mysterious way. He felt that if he were good enough, or persistent enough, she would pay more attention to him.

As a result of his early experiences with his mother, George learned two things. He associated his beloved mother's coolness with love and desirability, and he felt he was inadequate and unworthy. In order to feel worthy, he would have to win over a cool, aloof woman like his mother. Anyone else who might respond to him with warmth and acceptance wouldn't be good enough.

THE FICKLE LOVER

The Fickle Lover, like the Perfectionist and the Romanticist, can't commit herself to any one person. But instead of sequential relationships, she has simultaneous ones. She is afraid of putting too much faith in one lover, even temporarily. She needs a backup, so if her lover disappoints her, all is not lost.

The Fickle Lover can be either male or female, attractive or plain. Fickle Lovers are all good at keeping lovers on a string by appearing to make a commitment when they haven't and keeping their lovers interested in spite of their split loyalties. They usually appear very caring and devoted—to each lover in turn. The lovers may know about each other or one may know while the other is unaware. Occasionally a Fickle Lover keeps her secret from both of them.

What distinguishes these Distancers from others who have more than one lover is that they create the impression that each lover is their "one and only." They fully believe that they love each one equally and consciously try to choose between them. They believe, and their lovers believe, that they really want to settle down with one person. If one of the lovers (or both) becomes aware of the existence of a rival, he is made to feel that he is the favored one, and a breakup with the other lover is only a matter of time. He is led to believe that guilt, obligation, or neurotic need keeps the Fickle Lover from being totally his.

People who are attracted to Fickle Lovers often have their own problems with closeness, and a partially available lover satisfies their needs. For example, a Romanticist is often happy adoring a Fickle Lover. He would find her more desirable as a result of the insecurity of his relationship with her.

What makes it so difficult for the Fickle Lover to settle for one mate? She is usually very insecure and frightened of being alone. If she were to allow herself to love, want, and depend on only one person, she might be devastated if abandoned by him. By having two (or more) lovers, she insures herself against loneliness since if one lets her down, there will be another to love her.

A Fickle Lover may fear being controlled by her mate. If she has other lovers to turn to, she can avoid feeling too dependent on and vulnerable to any one person.

A Fickle Lover may feel so needy that she can't wait when she wants something. She may be easily frustrated and not feel that she has enough inner resources to satisfy her needs. Having two lovers makes it easier for her to ensure getting her needs met quickly.

Liz is a Fickle Lover. She is a single woman in her early thirties who had a prolonged affair with Bruce, a married man. For about three years, she dated other men as well, although she never got involved with any of them. Then she met Marty, a divorced man of about 40, and began to see him more frequently. She recalls, "I was very angry with Bruce at the time. He kept saying that he would leave his wife but kept putting it off. When he took her on a trip to Greece—the one I wanted to go on—it was the last straw."

Bruce became threatened by Liz's new involvement, left his wife, and asked Liz to move in with him. Her response was, "He left Barbara only because he thought he was losing me. It's too late; now I'm involved with Marty."

It seemed at that point that Liz was was finally willing to get involved with one man, whom she could marry. However, it didn't last. After several months of seeing only Marty, Liz began to miss Bruce. She said, "Maybe I was too hasty in dropping Bruce" and started seeing him secretly. Now the situation was reversed, with Liz having two men and Bruce being single and waiting. After about eight months, she broke up with Marty and moved in with Bruce.

This situation, also, was temporary. Within three months, she began seeing Marty on the sly. For two years Liz alternated between Marty and Bruce, often seeing both at the same time. When there were difficulties in her relationship with one of them, she turned to the other. When there were other stresses in her life, she would cling to both of them.

She said she really still loved Bruce—"He makes me feel alive." However, she complained that he worked too much and spent too much time with his children. She felt that she could never be "first" to him. Yet, by never committing to him, she avoided a role as his wife.

With Marty, she was "first." But although they had a lot of interests in common, after a while he seemed boring. She wanted them both and felt torn and guilty because of it.

Why couldn't Liz make up her mind? She was afraid to take a chance on either man because it meant giving up the other. She felt so afraid of being alone that she needed each one as backup for the other. If she married one of them, she would have only one to depend on. Her inability to completely trust either stood in the way of choosing one. Liz reacted to her fears by making sure she always had a safety net when she entered a relationship. She limited her dependence upon any of her lovers by having more than one relationship at the same time.

Why was Liz so afraid of being alone? Why couldn't she trust any one man to be there for her? Her mother was always disappointed in her. She wanted a feminine little girl dressed in petticoats and lace, but Liz was a tomboy. Liz said, "I always felt that I had to put on an act to please my mother," and when her mother was displeased, she acted as if she didn't love Liz. As a result, Liz grew up very untrusting of relationships. She was extremely compliant as a young girl, always afraid of displeasing teachers, other girls, and boys. When she grew into a beautiful teenager, she began to realize that men wanted her. She found that she could get their attention and approval by being flirty and seductive. "But," she said, "it was the same as it was with my mother—I always had to look and act the way they wanted." Although she played the game well, she constantly worried that they wouldn't stay with her if they found out what she was really like. By having two men all the time, she always had someone pursuing her and could always feel secure.

Liz had difficulty accepting these fears as the reason that she could not choose one of these men—or give them both up if neither was suitable. Most people like Liz do not readily admit that fear and insecurity motivate their behavior. They disguise their true feelings, tending to believe their defensive explanations. After Liz was able to see her fear for what it was, she could work on her basic insecurities and on taking a risk with one person.

THE OTHER WOMAN

Some people always seem to fall in love with married men or women in spite of hurtful outcomes. "All the good men are taken," Jane says, "and married men are so much more mature and giving." Yet they cannot give her what she says she wants—a family of her own. Why does she continue these affairs?

Women who are constantly having affairs with married men are sometimes variants of Romanticists. As long as their lovers are essentially unavailable, they can sustain their interest in them. An affair is always romantic and lends itself to fantasy. The Other Woman is free to idealize her lover and to blame any inadequacies she perceives in him on his spouse or the situation.

If an available man shows interest in the Other Woman, she will most likely dismiss him as undesirable. Like the Romanticist, she doesn't think well enough of herself to believe that a desirable and available man would love her. She may not see herself as deserving a man all her own.

Some Other Women feel safest with married men, whom they feel they have something over because the men don't want the affairs exposed. This offers Other Women a false sense of security that their lovers won't leave them.

For many women, having affairs with married men is preferable to marriage, since it offers them some measure of security without marital demands. They may have witnessed their fathers being very demanding of their mothers and consequently fear having husbands.

Sometimes these women avoid marriage because of strong parental ties. If their parents are overbearing or needy, they can't visualize themselves dealing with both the parents and a husband.

Women who have invested a great deal in their careers may be afraid that marriage will curtail their independence, causing them to lose their identity. In affairs they feel more in control. They can have their men and still have their freedom.

Jane is a 35-year-old manager of a computer company. Getting ahead in her career is very important to her. She recently began an affair with one of her colleagues, Gary. Their work had thrown them together during the day and often through dinner. They found that they understood each other and enjoyed being together. After a while, the quality of their relationship changed. For Gary, Jane was a welcome relief from his dependent, predictable wife. For Jane, it meant that she didn't have to choose between work and love.

Jane said, "I feel that I have the best of both worlds. Unlike some of my women friends, I can give my best to my work but still have a man in my life. Because he doesn't have any control over me, and I don't have any responsibilities toward him, I enjoy him more."

For many like Jane, intimacy is easier to handle in an affair than in a marriage. They find that the everyday contact and demands of a full-time relationship make them want to withdraw. In an affair they can control the amount of time spent with their lovers so that they are comfortable. They feel freer to be close because time limits the intensity of the relationship.

Intimacy in an affair is also easier because it offers less responsibility, fewer everyday problems, and more emphasis on enjoyment. Even when lovers talk about their problems, their expectations are different than in a marriage, so they have less resentment toward each other and little sense of being controlled or pressured. Affairs have built-in excuses for limiting time and commitments. As a result, the Other Woman can simply blame the circumstances, never considering her need for distance or her discomfort with too much intimacy.

THE AFFAIR SEEKER

A Fickle Lover who gets married without solving underlying problems may turn into an Affair Seeker. This Distancer often maintains the illusion of intimacy in his marriage, but always needs the other woman to dilute his relationships.

The Affair Seeker uses the other woman to limit his dependency on his wife. He may feel trapped by the demands of his family. Other men may work more hours or engage in sports or fitness activities as a way of coping, but he turns to other women. All of a sudden, he no longer finds his wife attractive, and a new woman (who may or may not be younger, brighter, or more attractive than his wife) seems so sexy. The new woman serves as a wedge between the Affair Seeker and his wife. He no longer depends completely on his wife for his emotional and sexual needs.

Often the other woman is very different from his wife—she may be independent and exciting, while his wife is clingy and dependent. He may feel too threatened to want to marry such an independent woman, but he is attracted to her. And he may feel more able to be open emotionally and verbally with his lover because he doesn't feel as vulnerable as he does with his wife. But time and circumstances limit his vulnerability and closeness.

Jay is an example of a man who always needed other women "to keep myself from feeling that I live my life only for my family." Throughout his 25-year marriage, he had many outside affairs and sexual encounters. Jay described how it all started. "After I was married for a few years and had two children, I began to feel trapped. My first reaction was to work more hours. I found myself calling home and if Anne wasn't in a good mood, I'd stay later at the office. Soon, I began asking my secretary to dinner . . . and then more." While none of the women mattered to him as much as his wife did, he cherished the freedom to come and go as he pleased, and to sleep with whom he pleased. This prevented him from feeling dependent on his wife and controlled by her demands.

Sometimes men turn to affairs because of difficulty in maintaining sexual interest in their wives. They find that they are no longer aroused by them, either after they get married or after they have children. Although they may love their wives and feel warm and protective toward them, they no longer see them as sexual beings. Sometimes these men are suffering from the "Madonna Complex." They see women as either Madonnas (virginal) or Whores (sexual objects). Once the women they love become their wives and the mothers of their children, they unconsciously associate them with their mothers and can no longer see them as sexual objects. The incest taboo, which is usually reserved for mothers and sisters, is evoked. The men are never consciously aware of the reasons for their loss of sexual desire. They may blame their wives, saying they spend too much time with the children or have lost their attractiveness. Many of these men do recognize, however, that they separate women into two categories—"nice girls" and "bad girls."

Men who suffer from the Madonna Complex usually had overly strong ties to their mothers. Because of this close contact, when they were developing their sexuality, they had to learn to severely inhibit their sexual drives in the presence of their mothers. They learned too well, for anyone who reminds them of their mothers evokes this same response—an inhibition of sexuality.

Women can have this problem too. Anyone who reminds them of their father, either physically or in behavior toward them, turns them off sexually. Their fathers may have been overly seductive when these women were teenagers or younger, arousing forbidden sexual feelings. So they learned to turn these feelings off so completely that men reminding them of their fathers also provoke inhibition of sexual impulses. They may have affairs because they cannot be turned on by their spouses. In order to allow themselves to become sexually aroused by someone, there must be a separation in their mind between them and "family."

Women sometimes have affairs because of other sexual problems in their marriage. In order to have an orgasm, the woman has to "let go"—to give up control for the moment. If she is angry with her husband or disappointed in him, then she might not allow herself to do this. Often these women can have an orgasm alone or with a relative stranger because they may feel there is nothing to lose.

Some women have affairs because they feel so needy and dependent on their spouses for other things that they refuse to depend on them for sex and affection as well. They gain a false sense of independence by satisfying themselves sexually outside the relationship.

Feelings of sexual or personal inadequacy can also lead to affairs. Such affairs may be a chronic problem from the start. Or they may develop when the Affair Seekers reach middle age and fear losing their attractiveness, which can happen as a result of their own basic insecurity or their spouses' inattention. The affairs or a series of sexual flings may thus serve to bolster their confidence in themselves. Sometimes Affair Seekers' spouses also have affairs—to "get even" or to repair their damaged self-esteem and let their mates know "how it feels."

Some Affair Seekers seem to be continually seeking the excitement of being in love. They get high on being in love and always seem to be looking for a "fix." Since they cannot sustain that feeling in a marriage, they turn to new and exciting relationships. They use affairs or sexual encounters as a way of acting out—running away from themselves and their anxieties. To them, sexual games take the place of other interests or hobbies.

Others have a very low tolerance for frustration. When minor or situational problems occur in their marriages, or when their spouses cannot or will not give them what they want, they run to others to fulfill their needs. (This is different from a situation in which a marriage does not fulfill a person's needs most of the time.) These people cannot wait or put up with any frustration of their desires.

Some Affair Seekers, like Fickle Lovers, use their lovers as backup. Because of their strong fears of abandonment, they feel that they need the security of another person. Without realizing why, they hold on to previous lovers, close opposite-sex friends, and current admirers. These people usually also have low frustration tolerance. They differ from the others in that they hold on to the lover even when the spouse is very giving and reassuring.

For some, having an affair is a hostile act. The underlying (and often unconscious) motivation of these Affair Seekers is a wish to humiliate people of the opposite sex. They may have been humiliated by their mothers or fathers as children and wished to humiliate them in return. Out of fear of retaliation, however, they may have hidden this impulse behind exaggerated devotion. By having a secret affair, while acting loving and devoted to their spouses, they can humiliate both their lovers and their spouses without overtly admitting their hostility.

THE FUNSEEKER

Funseekers, like adorable children, are frequently very attractive and charming because of their spontaneity, sensuousness, and openness to new experiences. They seem to enjoy each moment fully and are not bothered by mundane details that worry others, such as bills, problems, obligations, and responsibilities. They "hang loose."

But Funseekers can be exasperating, too. Their pleasure- and thrill-seeking can be carried to extremes. Sometimes they drink too much or use drugs—all in the guise of having a good time.

They can't wait for anything, be it food, sleep, or sex. Their intolerance of delays makes them very angry when anything—others' needs or traffic jams, for example—gets in their way. Decisions are often made impulsively, without taking future consequences into account, since the immediate moment is all that matters to them.

Funseekers usually don't feel in control of their lives. They haven't worked out their sense of identity so they can't plan for the future. As children, Funseekers may have been either over-indulged—with no limits set and no expectations made—or, conversely, not given enough love and attention. In either case, they were unable to internalize adult values of delayed gratification and frustration tolerance. Under their facade of fun and games, Funseekers are frequently very depressed. They don't feel good about themselves and their achievements and they cover up by escaping from reality. They want to focus on the present because they don't feel they have much of a future.

An example of an extreme Funseeker is Don, a wholesale shoe salesman in his mid-thirties. Don's job requires a lot of time on the road. When he is in town, he lives with Sally. Don is a charming, funloving man whom Sally adores. She says he makes her laugh and gets her out of herself. She is a very serious person and enjoys his lighthearted spirit.

Sally pays the bills and manages the household. Don gives her money sporadically—sometimes a great deal and sometimes nothing. She knows he spends his money impulsively on clothes and bets on horses. When he's home he rarely helps her, constantly putting off things that he doesn't want to do. When she tries to talk to him, he makes jokes and says she's too serious. She is concerned about their future together, but his attitude is "Not to worry." But she does worry—Don says she worries enough for both of them. She keeps hoping he'll change.

THE LONER

The most obvious distancer is the Loner. He can only sustain a relationship in which he can control the amount of time spent with his mate. He often can't consider her desires because of his strong needs to be alone.

The Loner becomes acutely uncomfortable, even anxious,

when he gets too close to someone. Since he is usually not aware of exactly what causes his discomfort, he attributes it to being "bored" with his lover or complains that she doesn't allow him his "space." To protect himself from his vague restlessness, he feels he has to "move on."

This type of Distancer often appears to be the strong, silent type. His mien of independence can be very appealing. He may be very successful in his career, especially if he can work alone or in a field in which he can limit his interaction with others or keep it superficial. Frequently, work is the major focus for a Loner, since it can be used as an escape from personal relationships. Financial success also allows him to accumulate possessions and pay for services, which serves to make him even more independent of others.

Sometimes successful career women are Loners. They may say that they want to get married but need to wait until their career is well established. These women may desperately want a relationship but are very fearful of too much closeness.

What are Loners so afraid of? Many are terrified of the responsibility of a spouse and children. They feel pressured by others and fear being depleted by others' demands. They may have received negative messages about marriage from their own family and see it as dangerous and diminishing.

Fear of being controlled by their mates can be the main problem for some Loners, while for others the main fear is being criticized. These IAs can stay involved only with someone who gives them total acceptance without criticism. While other Distancers also have these fears, the Loner is crippled by them.

Some Loners are so concerned with being controlled that they fear losing their "integrity" as a separate person. They have difficulty knowing who they are and what they stand for. Consequently, they fear being "swallowed up" by others or becoming an appendage to them. They fear that if they allow themselves to need and be needed by others they can no longer remain themselves. Women Loners particularly may see the demands of children and a husband as interfering with their own integrity.

Loners frequently get involved in limited relationships, especially when they are carefully pursued. If a Loner's partner doesn't expect much from him, and is willing to back off easily and quickly, he will feel less threatened and better able to become committed to her. However, he will always be self-protective and fearful of any hint of intrusiveness by his partner.

Loners rarely trust anyone to care about them and give to them. They most likely had poor relationships with their parents during their early childhood and never developed the security of having their needs met by others. They learned to insulate themselves from the pain of disappointment by minimizing their need for others. However, by becoming emotionally detached from lovers so that nothing will hurt or disappoint them, they choke off their emotional needs.

Jerry married Sue because she was quiet and undemanding. She didn't ask much from him, allowing him to spend his evenings silently watching TV or reading his newspaper. When her parents or friends visited, he would often go to his study to read and listen to music. Sue often felt neglected. "I wondered why he never talked to me, and why he avoided my family and friends. I was afraid to say anything to him about it because he would only pull away more." The situation became worse for her after they had a baby. Being home all day alone, caring for the baby with little support or companionship from Jerry, made her unhappy. She became so depressed that she sought therapy. After a few months, recognizing the impact of her marriage on her depression, she brought Jerry with her to sessions.

Sue and Jerry began to understand that he was a Loner, a very extreme sort of Distancer. He was afraid to get close to anyone. We wondered why.

Jerry's mother had died when he was 10. The family never discussed her illness and he never asked. "You just didn't ask my father about anything important," he said.

His father never remarried, and raised Jerry and his younger brother by himself. Jerry was always a "good boy" who never gave his father any trouble. He learned to "hold his feelings in" and never to depend on anyone else for emotional support.

Both Jerry and Sue realized that Jerry was afraid to depend on anyone and really didn't want anyone to depend on him— except perhaps for material things. When they were dating and then newly married, Sue didn't require very much from him. She still had her parents, her friends, and her colleagues at work. Now that she was home with a baby, she wanted more support and attention from Jerry. For their marriage to work, he had to learn, gradually, to trust and depend on her and allow her to depend on him emotionally. She had to proceed very slowly, always respecting his greater need for privacy and distance.

THE NARCISSIST

Narcissists are usually very appealing and desirable—on the surface. Typically attractive and well-groomed, they wear the latest fashions and spend a great deal of time staying in shape, eating right, and taking care of themselves. They place tremendous emphasis on looking good, going to the "in" places, and being with the "in" people.

These Distancers can be charming, knowing the right things to say to endear themselves to others. They are often bright, witty, and vivacious, and do great in public relations and sales. It is easy to get caught up with Narcissists—their tremendous confidence and enthusiasm are seductive.

However, it soon becomes clear to anyone who tries to get close to them that Narcissists are completely self-involved and totally absorbed with their own needs. They can be engaging and childlike, but like children they see themselves as the center of the universe. Having a grandiose sense of their own importance and worth, they exaggerate their success and have dreams of unlimited success, power, and wealth. They expect others to center their activities around them. If they don't, Narcissists are surprised and enraged. Because of their unusual sense of being entitled to things—they feel that everything is their due—they really can't understand why others don't cooperate with them. Anything done for them is minimized, and anything asked of them is exaggerated. They can't shift perspective to see things from others' viewpoints, so they are unable to consider their lovers' needs unless those needs coincide with their own.

Although they can't reciprocate, they require and expect constant nurturance and reassurance from others. If you join them in their self-admiration, they will reward you by idealizing you and sharing their pedestal with you. You will become part of their overinflated circle. But should you find the slightest fault with them—watch out. They will turn on you with a cruel vengeance. Narcissists will stay with lovers or friends only as long as it suits them. If things don't go their way, or if they feel their needs aren't being met, they drop those friends and lovers very quickly. Their utter callousness in discarding others is striking.

Behind the grandiose facade of the Narcissist is a fragile self-image. Narcissists need others' constant feeding, to ward off their underlying sense of emptiness and inadequacy. They literally can't take others' criticism, no matter how slight. When they don't get enough admiration from the world around them, they are prone to depression and feelings of vulnerability. They can become too concerned about their bodies, exaggerating every ache and pain to the point of being hypochondriacal.

We don't usually see the down side of the Narcissist, since most of them are clever enough to keep their supplies of admiration and attention going. If you are in a close relationship with one, however, you will see how easily he is wounded, by you and others. You might mistake this vulnerability for caring, but it is merely his ego that is hurt.

Narcissists didn't get their fair share of attention and positive feedback from their mothers when they were very young. They usually had mothers who were distant, cold, or self-involved and consequently didn't have enough to give. As children, the Narcissists never developed an internal sense of self-worth. Because their mothers were so unavailable, they compensated by pulling inward and investing their feelings in themselves. They never learned to get close to others.

Children who are emotionally deprived in their early years develop many different ways of coping. Those who are attractive and talented learn they can get recognition from the outside world. They perfect ways of gaining admiration from those around them while never truly caring about or developing empathy for others. Unfortunately, all the admiration they receive never makes up for what they lacked as children. A relationship with a Narcissist is burdensome. This is easily seen in the example that follows.

Cindy came for treatment because she was very depressed. (The only time a therapist sees Narcissists is when they are depressed.) She was a striking redhead, well-dressed, well-groomed, and beautifully made up—like the model she had been. Even at 59, Cindy was still a beauty. She was charming, appealing, and always onstage. She had been married twice, to men with a great deal of money, and now found herself almost broke because her last husband had gambled away his fortune. She left him and tried to make a life alone. Finding herself with no one to admire her—her whole social life had revolved around the big house and the social scene surrounding her husband's business—she became depressed. She was too old to go back to modeling and couldn't see herself working at anything else. She felt she needed to find a rich man who could give her the things she felt she deserved.

When she told me of her circumstances, I could sympathize with her loss and her plight. However, when she elaborated on how quickly she dropped her husband of 20 years because he had lost his money, I began to wonder about her and the sincerity of her feelings. Her husband had been gambling all along, but as long as his business covered his losses and he remained wealthy, she didn't care. When he could no longer support her in the manner in which she wanted to be supported, she left.

As therapy progressed, Cindy told of many escapades with men. She used men for sex, for admiration, and for social activities. After she felt comfortable enough with me to be completely frank, she laughed at what fools these men were. "I only want them to hang in my closet," she was fond of saying, "to have them there when I need them and then put them away." She didn't see any of these men as having lives or feelings of their own. They didn't mean anything to her, except as a way to meet her needs of the moment.

If a man had the gall to embarrass her or not go along with her wishes, she could be cruel in punishing him. She showed such callousness that at first I found it hard to believe she meant it. Was her behavior not hiding other, more tender or hurt feelings? But no, this was revenge, this was hate, this was pure and simple cruelty, with no holds barred because there was no ambivalence.

In most of us, no matter how angry we are at a beloved, there is a modulating effect of caring that prevents us from being too destructive. But in the Narcissist, as in a young child, there is no empathy. As a result, her revenge can be unbridled.

Cindy finally married again and left therapy. She no longer needed me. For the last time, I was struck by her lack of hesitation in severing a relationship that she no longer needed. Although everyone in therapy eventually leaves, it is always with some feelings of loss of the relationship. But for Cindy there was an utter lack of attachment to me. I felt strangely used at first, but I realized that I was dealing with a Narcissist.

⤮⤮⤮⤮⤮────────────────────────────

DISTANCERS, LIKE MOST PEOPLE, believe they are seeking intimacy. In reality, they are the most extreme of the Intimacy Avoiders in their evasion of closeness. In various ways they all manage to avoid becoming too attached to any one partner. Many of them never make a full commitment to one person, and those who do place great emotional barriers between themselves and their mates.

How do Distancers justify never making a commitment? Some are convinced that they haven't yet met the "right" person (Perfectionists), while others, such as Romanticists and Other Women, believe they have fallen in love with the "wrong" person.

Some Distancers are easier to spot than others. Loners, Funseekers, or Narcissists can be quite transparent (to others not involved with them) in their inability to form close relationships, while Fickle Lovers and Affair Seekers seem to get close too easily (and yet maintain distance by having more than one lover).

Regardless of what methods they use and what excuses they give, Distancers are evading real closeness in their relationships. They have the strongest fears of closeness of all the IAs. They are so afraid of being controlled, trusting others, or being criticized or otherwise betrayed or hurt, that they can't allow themselves to develop even the semblance of an intimate relationship.

3

Pseudo-Intimates

Pseudo-Intimates are more subtle than Distancers in their avoidance of intimacy. Although they sometimes have many of the same fears of closeness as Distancers, the intensity of their fears is not great enough to cause them to actively avoid commitment or split their loyalties between two partners. Pseudo-Intimates frequently commit to others and appear to outsiders to have good relationships. However, they place translucent veils between themselves and others. Their partners are usually aware of something missing but are unable to pinpoint the problem.

Pseudo-Intimates avoid being too close to their mates by becoming more involved with other people or activities outside their relationships, such as parents, children, friends, or work. The major distinguishing characteristic of Pseudo-Intimates is that these interests interfere with, and are used as a barrier to, intimacy with their mates.

DEVOTED CHILDREN OR DEVOTED PARENTS

Devoted Children   One way of appearing to be intimate while really having allegiances elsewhere is by being devoted to parents and never shifting primary allegiance to mates. When these Pseudo-Intimates have to make major decisions, they confer with their parents before their partners. And parents, rather than partners, are the first to hear of achievements, such as a raise or promotion, or disappointments, such as a fight with an employee or a friend. These Pseudo-Intimates spend inordinate amounts of time with their parents—seeing them every day or several times a week and speaking to them a great deal.

Their parents' wishes and needs are considered before their mates'. A Devoted Son might say, for example, that his elderly or sickly mother still needs him—to pay her bills, mow her lawn, paint her house, and so on. Or, he might say that she has gone through so much trouble to cook for him, how can he not stop over for dinner on his way home? She also does his shirts so well. His father is always so helpful with business problems, or fixing things around the house—they can't change a bulb without him. A Devoted Daughter, also, might need to help, or be nurtured by, mom or dad. Mom is needed for help with the children, for shopping, or cooking advice. And when the partners have an argument, the Devoted Daughter or Devoted Son has to run home to parents for comfort and advice. No wonder partners of Devoted Children often feel left out.

Why do Devoted Children still act like children? Sometimes they have difficulty separating from their parents because of feelings of obligation or guilt. These people may feel they owe a great deal to their mothers and fathers for all that their parents have done for them, given to them, or sacrificed for them. Devoted Children are often guilt-ridden, believing they have not been good enough and have to "make up" for past mistakes. Although these feelings can come about because of real sacrifices parents made for their children's education or because of great difficulties the children caused their parents when they were young, this type of guilt is not usually based on reality. In a reasonably good relationship, parents willingly give to the children without making them feel obligated or guilty. Even when there are unusual problems, either psychological or physical, parents need not make children feel guilty forever after. When they do, it is generally because of the parents' need to play the martyr in order to maintain control. The Devoted Child who allows this to make him feel guilty and obliged to "pay back," to his detriment and the detriment of his marriage, needs to see the situation for what it is and work out his feelings before they destroy his relationship.

Another reason that Devoted Sons or Daughters allow parents to interfere with their relationships is overdependence on them for money or approval. Needing or expecting financial help from parents causes Devoted Children to feel obligated to take their advice or do their bidding. If they require parents' approval, major decisions are not made without it. They often trust their parents' opinion and judgment more than they trust their own. Anything their parents say about their spouse, positive or negative, is seen as more valid than their own opinion. Even if they disagree, they frequently believe their parents know better.

Devoted Children invariably have parents who are overinvested in them and have difficulty letting go even after they have married. These parents frequently expect to have their own needs and desires considered ahead of those of their children's new family. They may attempt to maintain control by various manipulations or by instilling guilt. Some parents play up their illnesses, their age, their loneliness, or their financial need; others remind their offspring of all that was sacrificed for them. Parents such as these usually see spouses as rivals for their children's attention and constantly find fault with them, making married life very difficult for the younger couple. Blatant manipulation, such as when a mother-in-law openly criticizes or interferes, can be somewhat easier to deal with. Although very annoying, such behavior is easier for a couple to recognize and cope with. Subtle interference or manipulation is most destructive to a relationship and can be a source of great conflict in a marriage since it is often unrecognized by the son or daughter of the interfering parents.

Devoted Mother   Some people, especially women, are more intimate with their children than with their spouses. Although not unusual right after a baby is born, sometimes this imbalance continues throughout the child's life. In the guise of devoted mothers these women become intensely involved with their children, to the exclusion of the fathers. They may be reluctant to have sexual relations because "it might wake the baby" or they are "too tired from taking care of the baby." They avoid going out or on vacation alone with their husbands because they "can't leave the children." Their every thought and word is centered on their children's needs. When their husbands complain, these mothers say the husbands are jealous. They are! They have a right to be. Their children are taking all their wives' time and affection, leaving none for them. Typically, Devoted Mothers complain that their husbands don't spend enough time with the children. They are often right. What they don't see is their own contribution to the problem.

These women use their children as barriers between themselves and their husbands. Their husbands usually respond by spending more time at work, going out with friends, or withdrawing into television programs and newspapers. The couple may even fall into a comfortable pattern, never recognizing the lack of intimacy between them.

When her children grow up, a mother of this type feels a greater loss than most. She may try to cling to the children, becoming like the parents described above. If that fails, she may try to reach out to her husband, but he has usually adjusted his life to exclude her in many ways. At this point the couple usually reevaluates the relationship.

Devoted Mothers are generally the children of mothers who were more involved with them and their siblings than with their fathers. They never observed their parents relating to each other in an intimate way. Instead, their mothers made their relationships with their children primary. As adults, Devoted Mothers, like their own mothers, overinvest their energies and emotions in their children, to the exclusion of their husbands.

Some Devoted Mothers feel more secure being closer to their children—who are dependent on them and who therefore accept them unconditionally—than to their husbands. Others use their relationships with their children to work out issues that were unresolved with their own parents; by becoming better parents to their own children than their parents were to them, they vicariously obtain the nurturing they lacked. In either case, Devoted Mothers focus too much on their children and too little on their husbands, thereby interfering with intimacy in their marriages.

Devoted Dad This type of Pseudo-Intimate allows his children from a previous marriage to come between him and his beloved. He may never have resolved his feelings about his failed marriage and may be confused about his priorities. Usually divorced parents who are too involved with their children are guilt-ridden.

They may feel they abandoned the children when their marriage broke up—even if the former spouse initiated the divorce. Devoted Dads may have found it hard to separate from their own parents. When these men were children, they may even have felt abandoned by their parents—either physically or psychologically.

Fred is a 34-year-old divorced man with two children. He is seriously involved with Tracy. Although he has been seeing her for six months, she has never met his children, with whom he spends every weekend and every Wednesday evening. He tells her a great deal about them, but the children have never heard about her. He says that it would "upset" them and their mother if they thought that he was seeing anyone seriously. Tracy is distressed because Fred doesn't seem to be able to reconcile his previous life with the present. She worries that he won't be able to make future plans with her. On the other hand, she doesn't know what she can realistically expect from him. She can't ask him not to see his children, although she would like to. How can she determine what is reasonable?

Tracy is right to be concerned. She recognizes that although Fred needs to maintain contact with his children, he is leaving her out of the picture. She should expect him to tell his children about her and introduce her to them. Tracy should also be included in plans with the children, if she and Fred are ever going to have a future together. He is unable to let go of his past and is unwilling to accept that things have changed. He feels guilty about his divorce and about no longer living with his children. He will need to work out these feelings in order to enjoy the present and plan for the future.

THE WORKAHOLIC

The Workaholic is constantly involved with work of some sort. He usually enjoys his job and keeping busy, and may feel guilty when he isn't working. He puts in long hours at his job and seems always to be working when he's home—either on paperwork or chores. Or he is tired and needs to "mellow out."

Workaholics use work to insulate them from their mates, preferring the separateness that long hours of work provide. Since these IAs don't feel responsible for the hours they log, claiming their work is necessary, they avoid having to face their need for distance. The Workaholic's spouse often accepts the situation—even while complaining about being neglected—because her partner's success benefits both of them financially and socially.

While Workaholics strive to appear independent, they are often more dependent than they would like to believe. Their dependency is transferred to a boss, a company, or money and possessions.

Some amass wealth well beyond an amount they could ever use, usually in order to counteract feelings of deprivation and impoverishment. They are guaranteeing themselves that they will never need anyone for anything, that they can buy whatever they should ever require. Sometimes these people seem greedy—buying more than they can use, collecting books, paintings, or other valuable objects, or eating and drinking a great deal. They are giving to themselves to avoid wanting from others. Their need for acquisition is insatiable and compulsive because what they really need are love and approval, which they can't give themselves.

Frequently hidden under the cloak of superiority that many Workaholics wear are internal feelings of inadequacy. They require others' approval so much that they dare not risk the degradation they feel when they are not in a superior financial or social position. Their position protects them from the possibility of criticism or rejection, and their success affords them a sense of power that shields them from feelings of helplessness and insignificance. At work they feel in control whereas at home they may feel controlled by their spouse.

Workaholics have usually gained approval in the past through achievements rather than through relating to others. Many have not learned to be sensitive to others or to confide in them, and they feel awkward with closeness. But they feel comfortable and confident at work, where they know the rules and can be accepted. As a result, they usually choose to spend more time working than interacting with their families.

Sometimes Workaholics use their achievements or financial success as a means of winning love from their partners. They offer a bribe: "Look how wonderful I am, how much money I have . . . now will you love me?" They don't feel lovable for themselves and think they can insure love only through giving materially.

Doing well and making it financially became extremely important to the Workaholic in his childhood. Perhaps his father gave financial success priority and made achievement and high income his most important goals. Or perhaps his mother and family suffered because his father didn't do well and he vowed to never repeat this "failure" in his life. If he was raised in a successful neighborhood or had friends who had more than he had, his determination may be fired even more. Any of these situations can cause a child to grow up extremely determined—even driven—to do well at any cost.

Barry is a salesman for a major men's clothing manufacturer. In the past few years he has become one of the top salesmen in his company. By traveling a great deal and working long hours, he is able to give his family every advantage (advantages that he didn't grow up with). He doesn't understand why his wife, Sara, is protesting. Sara fears that Barry would rather be working than home with her and their children. She sometimes worries that he sees other women, but she consoles herself with the knowledge that he wouldn't take the time from work.

Barry feels that he needs to work as much as he does in order to "make a good living." But Sara says that he overdoes it and that they don't need so much money; they need him.

Is Barry avoiding intimacy by working, or does he really have to work so much? He, like other Workaholics, is more comfortable at work than in a close relationship. Although he tells himself that he has to work as much as he does, in reality he has chosen, albeit not consciously, to invest his sense of self totally in his achievements outside the family rather than in finding a balance between work and his relationship. Since he bases his self-esteem on how successful he is in business and how much he can provide for his family, he feels obligated to work a great deal. Barry's work provides him two major rewards—a sense of achievement, and protection from too much closeness with his wife.

Barry also uses his position as breadwinner to gain control in his marriage and with his children. When he wants something his way, he reminds Sara of how much his income provides for her. "What are you complaining about, you have everything you need—live-in help, beautiful clothes, a beautiful house, an expensive car. What more do you need?" And when he doesn't want to socialize with her or with friends, he says, "I work hard, I need my rest. If I don't work, nobody eats." This excuse has been overused and no longer has any effect on Sara. She rightly recognizes that he would rather work than relate on an intimate and equal basis.

MR. MACHO

Mr. Macho has to appear strong, powerful, and in charge, at all costs. He presents himself as superindependent, not allowing himself to admit needing anyone. A "real man" with an "I don't care" attitude, he can't indulge himself emotionally and won't indulge anyone else. Expressing feelings and needs is seen as weakness and despised. These men have a strong need to feel sure of their own versions of reality. They depend on their own efforts rather than trust others.

Mr. Machos act as if they know everything. They are generally highly productive in anything they undertake, being thorough and accurate thinkers who make careful plans and carry them through, no matter what the obstacles. They exude power and personal authority and make others feel needed very little, if at all. Being involved with one of these men can be very demoralizing because he leaves no room for anyone else's judgment and input and is often condescending to those who try to help him or offer suggestions.

Although right in their judgment about many things, Mr. Machos sometimes make mistakes. However, since they have to believe that they are infallible, they refuse to listen to anyone else or to acknowledge their mistakes. Instead they forge ahead with absolute certainty toward whatever they have decided to do—whether it is investing money or buying a house—and as a result, their mistakes can be very costly. Rather than take responsibility when things go wrong, they frequently blame their mates, saying that they "screwed up" the plans in one way or another.

Mr. Macho fights constantly for his own way *exactly*. Needing to be right all the time, he becomes irritated if proved wrong, even if only in a minor point. He can never give in because he sees agreeing with someone or accepting advice as a weakness. As a result, he seems to lean over backwards to avoid agreement and may even compulsively adopt an opposite position from his mate's, regardless of its validity.

Mr. Machos who are successful at their work frequently believe they are experts in every other area. So, for example, they act as if they know more than the doctor, the lawyer, the accountant, and anyone else they or their partners may consult.

Even those Mr. Machos who are not proficient in their jobs may act as if they know everything and speak with great authority about things of which they have little or inaccurate knowledge. They seek admiration and respect, but don't realize how little they know. Partners of such men are often very embarrassed by them.

Mr. Macho needs to feel in control at all costs, so he tries to anticipate every possible result of anything he undertakes and avoids situations involving risk or uncontrollable circumstances. Any kind of delay—traffic, red tape, others' needs—makes him impatient. Even falling in love causes him grief because he feels out of control. This anxiety sometimes turns to anger and contempt for his beloved.

Men such as these often marry Clingers (described in the next chapter) who won't leave them. And although they complain about such spouses spending too much money or messing up the check book, Mr. Machos become threatened if their "incompetent" wives try do anything for themselves, such as getting a job or going to school.

Although they may deny it, Mr. Machos attempt to control their mates. Sometimes this tendency to dominate is concealed in socially valuable ways—managing family affairs, giving advice, doing for others. For example, a Mr. Macho may appear to allow his wife to have total autonomy while insisting on discussing everything she plans to do. He may make decisions for both of them, assuming he knows what she likes. Mr. Machos can't have a relationship as equals. If they aren't completely in charge, they feel subjugated. When frustrated they tend to show their hostility by humiliating or depriving their mates.

Much of Mr. Macho's facade of strength is a protection against feelings of helplessness. To guard against seeing himself as weak in any way, he develops a rigid and irrational ideal of strength. He refuses to accept nurturance or help when appropriate.

Mr. Macho shows inflated pride at being able to master anything and sees a show of weakness as a disgrace and a danger. He sees people as either strong or weak, and those who show emotions or who give in to him or who even agree with him are weak and thus contemptible to him. He despises these same qualities in himself and feels humiliated if he has to recognize his own inhibitions or anxieties.

It is difficult, if not impossible, to have truly intimate relationships with Mr. Machos. Since they are totally invested in maintaining their power and dominance, which are central to their self-image, they are incapable of having anything resembling an equitable relationship. They need to maintain their image of strength, even in their most primary relationships, so they can't afford to allow themselves to be self-disclosing, spontaneous, or vulnerable. Nor can they be sensitive to their spouses' needs. As a result, mates of Mr. Machos may see them as "big strong men" and feel safe and protected, but they don't feel close to them.

A perfect example of a Mr. Macho is provided by Bob. He had been a marine during his early twenties, and in many ways he prides himself on still being like a marine—tough and independent. His wife, Connie, is soft, sweet, and dependent. Although others suspect that he likes her that way so he can always be the boss, he denies it. He complains that she isn't "tough enough" and that she expects too much emotional support from him.

Bob is a vice president of a small company. At work he is known as a stickler who demands that all work be methodically and precisely done. He is very hard on those who work for him, but he gets results.

Connie complains that Bob tries to run things at home the way he does at the office. He expects instant obedience from their children, especially their son, and often from her as well. Bob never admits he's wrong. Connie says he always wants his own way, on even the smallest matters such as where they eat or what she wears. Although he says he doesn't want to tell her what to do, he insists on knowing what she is doing at all times, often calling during the day to check up on her.

For many years Connie put up with Bob's bossiness because she felt dependent and fearful. But her expectations changed when their children became old enough to need her less and she decided to begin a career of her own. She had always wanted to be a commercial artist but gave it up because Bob insisted she stay home with the children. Now she felt she could pursue this goal. Bob was unsupportive, however. He made comments like, "It's costing me plenty to send you to work—taxes, household help, and your clothes cost more than you earn." When she got a raise he said, "My bonus is more than your whole salary." It was clear that he didn't want her to become independent in any way. Connie became aware that if she wanted to become independent, she would have to find support from others rather than her husband.

THE RESCUER

Rescuers are wonderful to have as friends when you have problems. They are extremely empathic listeners, offering help, advice, and concern. They thrive on taking care of others and rescuing them from difficult situations.

It is difficult to fault Rescuers, since they are so giving and caring, but they are true Pseudo-Intimates. By concentrating completely on their mate's problems, feelings, and vulnerabilities, they manage to keep themselves insulated and protected. Unable to admit their own dependent yearnings or even their own realistic need for nurturance, they insure that they are indispensable by making their mates dependent on them.

Rescuers feel comfortable being in the giving role but threatened when others want to give to them. Acknowledging their fears, vulnerabilities, or needs to others makes them anxious and guilt-ridden. They don't want to be in a position where they owe their partners anything; they would rather have it the other way around. After a while, though, many partners feel bad about always taking and never having the satisfaction of giving back.

Rescuers are usually competent and giving people who as children were required to take care of their parents' and younger siblings' emotional needs. Since their parents couldn't provide emotional support for them, they grew up feeling guilty taking from others. They were brought up to believe they were strong and able to handle anything alone. Expecting others to be incapable of giving to them makes them fear needing anyone else.

By identifying with their partners, Rescuers get vicarious satisfaction from nurturing them. Thus, they may sometimes give their partners what they themselves want, rather than what their partners want, and they may become disappointed and hurt if their efforts are not fully appreciated.

Sometimes Rescuers avoid intimacy by marrying neurotic people who cannot either function by themselves or participate in a real relationship. They then see themselves as good, caring people who want more closeness but can't have it because their spouses are "sick." But if the spouses became better, the Rescuers would have to face their own fears of closeness.

As with all relationships that pair a more controlling but giving partner with a weaker one, the balance is tenuous. If the weaker, overtly dependent spouse becomes stronger, the status quo is threatened. As a result, Rescuers, who are invested in their partners' need for them, often sabotage their partners' growth.

Chris appears to be the perfect mate. Her boyfriends can always talk to her about their problems. She is always patient, always understanding, always helpful. Chris will go to enormous trouble to help out her mate, but she never admits to any problems herself. She hides her own difficulties behind a facade of cheerfulness and competence.

Chris is a nurse and enjoys taking care of others in her work and in her relationships. When she was growing up, she helped her mother care for her younger brothers and sisters. She was always the "good girl." She didn't feel that there was any room for her to be needy. By taking care of her siblings, she gained her mother's approval, and by identifying with them, she could vicariously enjoy her own nurturing.

To some she seems ideal, but many men have begun to feel uncomfortable with her all-giving superindependent attitude. She seems too good to be true and in fact doesn't allow anyone to get close enough to see any of her disappointments, her faults, or her pain. She is afraid that, like her mother, who was overwhelmed with five young children, her partners won't be able to handle or accept her needs.

THE INTELLECTUALIZER

The Intellectualizer is the consummate Pseudo-Intimate—he plays out his part perfectly. Considered by others "a good husband," he not only provides for his family, but spends time with the children—taking them to the park, helping put them to bed, generally involving himself in their lives. He always remembers birthdays and anniversaries, never failing to provide the appropriate gifts and cards.

Why is he a Pseudo-Intimate? Because in spite of his perfect performance, he is emotionally unavailable. He may do all the right things and look good on the surface, but he is stiff, formal, and overly serious. Preoccupied with logic, intellect, and rules, he doesn't have time for fun or pleasure. Consequently, he takes the children to the zoo or museum for educational purposes, not for enjoyment.

His mate never knows what he really feels because expressing feelings or affection is foreign to him and any attempts to do so seem awkward and artificial. The Intellectualizer is not in touch with his feelings. Like a Rescuer, he doesn't want to be vulnerable, but unlike a Rescuer, who is sensitive and responsive to a mate's emotions, he isn't tolerant of his mate's expression of feeling. Since he is overly moralistic, believing that everyone should be contained at all times, he may even become angry when she wants to express affection or resentment.

The Intellectualizer has an inordinate need for control—of himself, others, and the situation around him. Because he needs to do the "right thing" all the time, he has difficulty making decisions, forever analyzing every option. He needs everything to be in order, in its place, so that he can feel comfortable. As a result, he has difficulty tolerating change and can be extremely unyielding and obstinate when his mate wants to depart from the usual procedure, whether in household routines or lovemaking.

The Intellectualizer can be self-righteous morally and intellectually. Although perfectionistic and critical of others, he doesn't always censure or complain openly as the Constant Critic (described in the next chapter) does. Rather than express his anger or disapproval directly, he tends to show quiet contempt for his mate when she doesn't conform.

Eric is a successful accountant. He is always neatly groomed and dressed and appears to have everything under control. His wife, Jenny, complains that he is rigid in the way he expects her to run the house and keep the children, and in their personal relationship.

Although Eric appears appropriately attentive to his wife and children, he lacks emotional involvement with them. He tries, but finds it very difficult to express warmth and affection. He doesn't like to be touched and gets close to his wife only when he wants sex. When Jenny becomes upset with this, she says that maybe sex is all he needs, that he really doesn't love her. At other times she says she believes he cares for her, but can't feel it from him—he is too blocked in his feelings and keeps too much inside. Jenny's other complaint against Eric is that he never seems to want to have fun. Whenever she tries to plan a vacation or even an evening out, he finds a reason to put it off. He will plan all the details of a trip with her, for instance, but then keep delaying it until the "right time." If she complains too much, or gets too upset with him, he calls her "hysterical" and merely walks away. She stays with him because he is basically a good husband and she loves him. Yet she wishes that he could "loosen up."

THE SOCIAL BUTTERFLY

Socializing with others, individually and as a couple, is part of every relationship, but some IAs *always* seem to need a crowd around them. Their socializing is sometimes with family members, sometimes with friends or business contacts. While they have many acceptable reasons for all this social activity, the bottom line is that IAs hardly ever find time to be alone with their partners.

Some women become tied up with various daily social activities—bridge, shopping, lunch, the spa. This is fine if their relationships with their children and their husband do not suffer. The woman who is a Social Butterfly, however, uses these activities and her relationships with her friends as a substitute for an intimate relationship with her husband.

Male Butterflies may spend a great deal of time in the gym,

on the court or the golf course, or "out with the boys." They are unconsciously substituting contacts with their buddies for their relationship with their wives.

Social Butterflies seem to fear being alone with their mates. Their subjective assessment is that they are bored and want constant stimulation. They say they don't want to be "couch potatoes" and wither: they need to keep busy and interested.

Many of these people are afraid to deal with closeness or vulnerability. They fear trusting one person to keep them interested and they fight loneliness and emptiness by surrounding themselves with many people. As a result, they close off intimacy with sociability.

A variant of the Social Butterfly is the Good Friend. She is closer to her "best friend," male or female, than to her husband or lover. Sometimes the friend is a male colleague with whom the woman is having an emotional affair. She is often unaware that she is more intimate with him than with her husband. Her friend frequently has more in common with her and understands the daily pressures and stress of work or school better than her husband does.

The Good Friend may be a close female friend or neighbor, who shares her daily life and with whom she shares deep feelings—fears, hopes, desires. The women frequently spend most of their day together and then socialize in the evening and on weekends with their husbands. They may go on vacations together and completely share their lives. Husbands of these women have no choice at all about the friendship. They may complain, but feel foolish being jealous of their wives' best friend. They usually don't realize that their envy of the intimacy between the women, which substitutes for the intimacy in their marriage, is justified.

Some Good Friends are like Affair Seekers or Fickle Lovers, who need to create a buffer in their relationships with their partners by having additional intimates. They may be very close to their friends but are able to sustain this closeness only because it is limited.

Other Good Friends are actually seeking intimacy but have given up on their spouses. Although choosing to stay in their marriages for any number of reasons, they look outward for true intimacy. While it isn't exactly accurate to call them Intimacy Avoiders, they are avoiding closeness, or the possibility of it, with their spouses.

Heather is a Social Butterfly. A great hostess, she entertains her husband Bob's clients and has proved to be quite an asset to his business. She has lots of friends and leads an active social life, and she is involved with her women's groups and many other activities. But she rarely has time for a quiet dinner with Bob. He complains that they are never alone together. Whenever he wants to spend time with just her, she has an engagement or has invited people to their home.

Heather has surrounded herself with friends since she was young. She feels secure knowing that if one friend is not available, she can call others. Although she says she is close to her friends, there seem to be too many for actual intimacy. She talks to them about the daily incidents of her life but rarely discusses feelings or deep thoughts with anyone.

Bob is very much involved with his business, so he doesn't often notice that there is little closeness in their relationship. However, he has occasionally wondered why Heather seems to avoid being alone with him.

THE STATUS SEEKER

The most important thing to the Status Seeker is what friends, neighbors, and the rest of the world think of her. Taking her mate for granted, she looks outside for respect and appreciation. She needs constant approbation to fill a void within her and to repair her crushed self-esteem. As a result, she might spend more time doing things for the community—working on a town board or doing charity work for the local church or school—than for her own family.

The Status Seeker may appear to be close in her relationships if she thinks it is important for her image. She tends to put on a show so that friends and relations will think she has the perfect marriage. And, as far as she is concerned, her marriage is fine. As long as there aren't many disagreements or conflicts, things are satisfactory. However, there is no time for intimacy. She is too busy trying to win approval from the world. Since outsiders don't require her to be open and emotionally available, she feels more comfortable with the superficial relationships they offer.

Lacking security within herself, she requires external trappings to bolster her ego. In order to feel better about herself as well as to impress others, she buys expensive clothes, cars, homes, and furniture. She frequently uses her children and spouse to impress others. Her husband's success at work is a source of bragging and status to her. Where the children go to school, how they do, and whom they play with are all used to gain acceptance and respect from others.

Male Status Seekers often show off their wives, buying them expensive presents like diamond rings and mink coats. Their wives thus become expensive accessories or pets for them.

If the Status Seeker marries a Workaholic or other Pseudo-Intimate primarily because of his financial and social success, she may be very disappointed in his other qualities. As described in the earlier section on Workaholics, the qualities that make him so financially successful also may make him less available. While some Status Seekers may not mind this distance—as long as their status needs are met—others might feel slighted and neglected.

Since their self-esteem is so vulnerable and others' opinions so important, Status Seekers are excessively sensitive to humiliations. They are not always aware of feeling humiliated but when small shortcomings are brought to their attention, they react with disproportionate rage—in private situations with their mates and, even more, if the perceived insults or complaints are made in front of others.

Arlene and Frank exemplify the Status Seekers. He is an attorney and she is a school teacher. They are two competent people who for all the world appear to have the perfect marriage. They live in a good neighborhood, in a beautifully maintained home. They entertain frequently and have a reputation for being gracious hosts. In their daily life they have everything worked out—sharing the expenses, housework, cooking, and responsibilities toward the children. Their children are enrolled in the "best" schools and they drive a Jeep, the "latest" car in their neighborhood.

Both of them are heavily involved in community affairs.

Frank is on several political committees, while Arlene is in the PTA and three women's groups. They lead a very active social life. In spite of all of this, neither Frank nor Arlene is happy. Why? You guessed it—there is no real intimacy! On the surface all is fine, but they speak to each other about superficial things, never about their feelings. These people care about each other; you could even say that they love each other. But neither one of them feels free to be close. Each is more concerned with what others think and their reputation in the community.

Arlene began to feel depressed at one point. At the recommendation of her friends, she came for psychotherapy. Although at first her defenses covered them up, after a while her feelings of insecurity and inadequacy surfaced. Looking at her family background helped clarify why she always felt the need to please outsiders while being afraid to get too close to her husband.

Arlene was the only child in large extended household of her parents, her grandmother, and her mother's brothers and sisters. She was the center of attention but didn't feel genuinely cared about by the family. Rather, she felt "used" by them for their entertainment. As a child, she was pretty and cute and was made to show off and perform for the family and their guests. Her father was even more hurtful than the others. He expected her respect and obedience, but he often ignored her or rejected her openly. The family demanded affection when they wanted it, but were too busy for her when she needed them. Arlene grew up feeling that she always had to perform to be accepted.

As an adult, Arlene acts as if she will be liked only if she always does the "right" thing. She is extremely dependent on recognition, spending too much time and energy looking outside the family for it. With time, Arlene learned to understand the reasons for her feelings—why she needs so much acceptance and why she is so afraid of rejection from a man that she dare not risk getting too close to her husband. Because of Frank's needs for distance and for outside approval, Frank and Arlene unwittingly collude to keep their marriage picture perfect but distant. In order for them to change the nature of their relationship, they have to break down barriers of fear and allow each other to get close.

THE CONSTANT COMPETITOR

Constant Competitors are usually successful business or professional people who carry their competition and aggressiveness into their relationships. In the past, they were almost always men, but now they can just as easily be women.

Competitors feel rivalry with their partners, sometimes trying to defeat or frustrate their partners' efforts. Successful men whose wives begin to do well at work may adopt the attitude that "only one can succeed" and feel uncomfortable when their wives seem to be catching up or surpassing them in any way—financially, educationally, or socially.

Constant Competitors have difficulty switching from attitudes necessary in business situations to those more appropriate to intimate relationships. When the Constant Competitor comes home, he has to change gears. He has to consider his partner's needs as well as his own and work in a compromising and cooperative way. This is particularly difficult for men, since they often have little training in compromise. If they see their wives as dependent on them, they are able to treat them protectively, but if the women become equal in status, perhaps even outdoing them, the male rivalrous spirit is aroused.

Constant Competitors also choose partners with an eye toward winning out over others. Women, in particular, will try to marry a successful man so as to compete with their friends and acquaintances. However, sometimes when a very competitive woman marries a successful man, she is in conflict. On the one hand, she loves her husband for his success but, on the other hand, she hates him for it. His achievement makes her successful in the eyes of other women and society, but because she is competitive with him she feels inadequate by comparison. She might want to destroy his success but can't because she enjoys it vicariously and participates in the rewards it offers. So she shows her admiration on the surface and takes out her resentment by looking for small things to criticize him for and by an insidious disparaging attitude. This attitude becomes clearest at any sign of failure, when, rather than being supportive and encouraging, she turns on him and becomes critical of past and current behavior.

Some wives get even by becoming extravagant, endangering their husbands' financial security and putting down their achievements by wasting the rewards. By buying more and more expensive clothes, cars, or other conspicuous items, they also increase their own self-esteem. Whatever the means, the end results are competition and envy rather than intimacy.

Nancy is a housewife married to John, a successful attorney. She says she is very proud of her husband's achievements and his recent partnership in a large, prestigious law firm. However, she seems to subvert his success by sometimes making subtle negative comments about him when they are out with his clients or law partners. She is quick to point out any fault of his, even in front of others. John has begun to suspect that she is jealous of his success and competitive with him.

When he was having a difficult time with a very important case, Nancy was unsupportive and used every opportunity to find fault with whatever he did. She made it hard for him to spend time at home working on his briefs, saying he never spent time with the children. Although she may have been right, her timing was terrible.

When we explored this in therapy, she at first denied any attempts to subvert his success but later was able to admit her envy of his position. She felt angry because she was the one who gave up graduate school for work while he finished law school. Then she was home with young children. Now she felt that going back to school would be too much of a burden for her to handle along with running the house.

Nancy had to realize that her envy of her husband was causing barriers between them. She needed to work on her own inability to achieve what she wanted for herself so that she no longer brought her feelings of inadequacy and inferiority into her marriage.

❦❦❦❦

AS THE DESCRIPTIONS of the various types of Pseudo-Intimates illustrate, each has characteristic ways of subtly avoiding closeness with a mate. Unlike Distancers, who more obviously and actively set up excuses for avoiding total commitment to potential mates, Pseudo-Intimates make commitments but dilute their relationships by getting too involved with outside interests. Some of the Pseudo-Intimates invest too heavily in their relationships with their parents or children (Devoted Parents and Children), while others give first place to their friends, acquaintances, or the community (Social Butterflies and Status Seekers). The other Pseudo-Intimates—the Workaholics, Mr. Machos, Rescuers, Competitors, and Intellectualizers—allow their quest for power, dominance, status, or superiority to substitute for, and stand in the way of, closeness with their partners. Other people may have strong needs for power, status, or achievement, but they integrate their work or community activities with their relationships. Pseudo-Intimates, however, use their jobs or outside interests as a substitute for closeness with their mates. They may want and need intimacy as everyone else does, but their fears of closeness cause them to hide their desires, even from themselves, and invest their emotional energies in other things. These fears, although preventing real intimacy, are not as strong as those of Distancers. As a result, Pseudo-Intimates generally have a greater degree of connection to their partners than Distancers and are much more subtle in their evasion of closeness.

4

Intimacy Saboteurs

Intimacy Saboteurs are different from other Intimacy Avoiders. They don't try to avoid closeness at all. In fact, most of them are very dependent and want the security of an intimate involvement. However, true intimacy eludes them because of the way they relate to their mates. Rather than backing away—either overtly or subtly as Distancers and Pseudo-Intimates do—they cause others to want to distance from them. They consciously want to be close, but make it uncomfortable for their mates to be close to them. Each type of Intimacy Saboteur has a characteristic style of pushing mates away. Let's see how they do this.

THE CONSTANT CRITIC

The Constant Critic sabotages intimacy in his relationships by being too exacting in his expectations of his mate. In most situations, he demands more than is required, and he is relentless in his criticism when his standards are not met. He has very strong opinions of how others should act and finds it difficult to see things from his partner's perspective.

While some Critics seem to be harder on their mates than on themselves, many are equally unrelenting with their own behavior. They are similar to perfectionists but fear closeness less. They don't use their high standards to avoid getting involved or choosing a mate. Instead they choose mates whom they spend their lives attempting to reform by constant nagging and put-downs.

The Constant Critic finds fault with everything his partner does. He emphasizes and remembers more negative things about his partner than positive. Because he is so focused on perfection and detail, he often loses perspective and is unable to distinguish between minor details and major flaws. As a result, any little flaw in his mate or in what his mate does is interpreted as "ruining the whole thing." Since anything can be done more efficiently, or better, he is rarely satisfied with how his mate performs.

Critics vary in their methods of rebuke. Some are subtle—hiding behind a cover of friendliness while they take pot shots at their mates. They use innuendos, nonplayful teasing, and subtle and not-so-subtle digs. For example, a Critic might scrutinize everything his mate does, making snide comments about the fin-ished product or her inefficiency or slowness. He might say he's kidding and call her "slowpoke" or "butterfingers." Another Critic, pretending to be "helpful," might be less than supportive when his mate tells him about an incident that upset her. He might a priori assume that she is overreacting or that she handled the situation badly. Some Critics don't censure their partners outright but make faces when their partners are telling stories; others will contradict whatever their partners say. Critics can be also be humorous and sarcastic, making jokes to others about their mates. Sometimes Constant Critics are so artful in their approach that their partners aren't sure they are being attacked. For ex-ample, one Critic loved to say about his wife, "You can always find Judy when you need her; just have her paged at Bloomie's."

Complainers are a variant of the Constant Critic. They gripe about everything, from the weather to the messiness of the house. The disguised message is that someone, usually their partners, should be doing something about it. They put their partners on the defensive. It's difficult to sort out their legitimate complaints from their constant fault-finding. They have an accusatory style that makes others feel in the wrong. While they may choose issues that have some substance to them, Complainers, like other Con-stant Critics, are very picky.

Their partners tend to react to Complainers by becoming defensive or placating. For instance, one woman whose husband complains about her spending tries to justify whatever she buys, continually explaining why she needs the clothes or whatever else she bought. Sometimes, she just doesn't mention her purchases to her husband, or says the money was spent for the children. These partners don't really try to solve the problem, which at times is real, because they are so used to the others' complaining.

Rather than reproach their partners directly, some Complainers talk about them to parents, children, or friends. These Complainers are afraid of direct confrontation and wait until they feel safe—when others are around and their mates are less likely to respond with anger—to state their gripes. They are also looking for support and sympathy from others. This public griping is particularly destructive since it serves to make the partner feel inadequate and humiliated at the same time.

Constant Critics are difficult to live with also because they pressure themselves as well as those around them. They are often unhappy with themselves and depressed. One woman said, "I drove my husband nuts—anytime he dropped an ash in an ashtray, I ran after him. I finally let him use one ashtray. I dreaded entertaining, and always felt pressured, and complained that my husband was not cooperative or helpful. He could never clean or set up anything the way I expected."

Why do they need to criticize others so much? Constant Critics have very strong consciences and ideals. They have an image of how things ought to be, and they feel angry with others—especially their mates—for not conforming to their expectations. Critics feel that by consistently pointing out what they see as their mates' deficiencies, they will influence their mates to change.

As with the Perfectionist, the Constant Critic sees his partner as a reflection of himself and his status, which is seen by the rest of the world. He doesn't want anyone to find fault with him or anyone associated with him.

Some, especially the complainers, feel powerless to manage their own lives. They believe the only way to get things done is to have others pay attention and take action. Their complaining takes the burden off them so that they appear, to themselves and others, blameless and innocent. Having brought the problems to their partners' attention, it becomes the partners' responsibility.

Constant Critics were usually sensitive and insecure children. They probably tried to win approval from the kind of parents who were very difficult to please. These parents rarely give praise but always expect more, keeping their children reaching on tiptoes; they withhold full acceptance in an attempt to urge their children to do better. If the children try hard in school and earn grades of B or B-plus, the parents ask for A's. If the children clean up their rooms, the parents say the rooms aren't clean enough. When these children become adults, they can never be good enough to please the parents in themselves. As adults, Constant Critics act toward their partners and children the same way their parents acted: never satisfied, always expecting better, and constantly withholding approval.

June is a Constant Critic. She finds fault with her husband Stan, saying he doesn't help enough at home. When he tries to help, she chastises him for the way he does things—especially when he is dealing with the children. She doesn't like the way he runs his business and regularly tells him so: he should be stricter with his employees, he shouldn't be as lenient with them about time off, he pays them too much, and so on. Stan often jokes that perhaps he should stay home and she should run the business, but she says she already has too much to do at home. After a while, Stan stops listening to June. She complains that he ignores her, but can you blame him?

June is as much a perfectionist with herself (and the children) as she is with Stan. She expects a great deal of herself as a mother, as a homemaker, and in her work with women's organizations. She has very strong feelings about how things "should" be and how people "should" behave. When others, especially those in her family, don't comply with these unspoken standards, she becomes very upset. She says that if she doesn't watch them to make sure they do things the "right" way, they will "mess up everything."

June's mother was very unemotional, rarely expressing affection or approval. When June was a child, her mother expected her to keep her dresses clean when she went out to play. If June got dirty, her mother would become angry with her. June was always expected to do well in school and to perform her chores perfectly. Her mother had no patience with childish efforts or incomplete tasks. June internalized these standards as well as her mother's general dissatisfaction with what others could do for her. She carried this into her marriage.

THE SENSITIVE SULKER

Oversensitivity to others' reactions is the hallmark of the Sensitive Sulker. She may be able to take care of herself and support herself financially, but she depends on others for her self-esteem. Underneath it all, the Sensitive Sulker feels bad about herself. Consequently, she expects her mate to judge her as harshly as she judges herself. Anticipating reproofs and rebuffs, she is constantly on the defensive, warding them off. At the slightest suggestion of criticism, she pulls away, teary and hurt. Her message is "Don't hurt poor little me or I'll get depressed and it will be your fault." By withdrawing from her mate and making him feel guilty for hurting her, she manipulates him. Sensitive Sulkers usually choose partners who are susceptible to their tactics. These partners are probably fearful of being rejected themselves or are overly concerned about hurting others.

The Sensitive Sulker's extreme fear of rejection causes her to interpret any attention her mate pays to others as neglect of her, and any comments that are less than totally positive as a humiliation. Her fear of rejection can also cause her to become distant and withholding at times, since she is unwilling to put herself in a position to be rejected.

Sensitive Sulkers are generally insecure, frightened people. They may have been overly sensitive children who were not given enough comfort or reassurance when they felt inadequate. Usually their parents didn't encourage them to build their self-esteem, either because it threatened the parents or because they basically didn't approve of their children's behavior. Some Sensitive Sulkers were openly disapproved of or rejected as children. When they reacted by becoming angry and demanding or by withdrawing, their parents may have rejected them further. As a result, these children grew up feeling insecure about being accepted and loved.

They have deep inner fears about their basic lovability and "goodness" as people. Although many try to compensate for these feelings about themselves through high achievement, or cover them up with bravado and apparent confidence, their inner fears still remain.

Children react to disapproving parents in many ways. Those who become Sensitive Sulkers are usually more capable of functioning on their own and so are able to withdraw without feeling devastated. And since by temperament these children are not compliant, they don't try to gain approval by greater attempts to please.

Judy is a Sensitive Sulker. She appears competent and independent. She is an attorney for a large, successful law firm and earns as much money as her husband, John. In her relationships with clients and colleagues, she is quite effective. But at home with John, she acts differently. She is very touchy and easily hurt by any hint of criticism or less than total acceptance from him. When she isn't given all his attention, she feels rejected and left out.

Judy is threatened by John's relationships with others—even their teen-aged daughter. If the girl appears to prefer her father in any way, Judy is jealous of her daughter's affection as well as her husband's. She has come to understand that her overreactions are irrational but she cannot control them. She still feels hurt and rejected and usually shows it by withdrawing from her family. They react by turning to each other, confirming her feelings of being left out.

THE PEOPLE PLEASER

People Pleasers appear to be genial, good people who try, at all costs, to please their mates. They are compliant in order to win and hold affection, so they can't feel secure unless they continually submit to their partners' wishes.

Usually considered easygoing, People Pleasers act as if it doesn't matter to them what they do, where they eat, and so on. It is hard to imagine that nothing matters to them; what is more likely is that keeping their mates happy is more important to them than having their own way.

Partners of People Pleasers rarely complain that the People Pleasers are too compliant with them, but they are frequently disturbed by the People Pleasers' need to please others—bosses, colleagues, neighbors, parents, children, or subordinates. Because they need to be liked by everyone, People Pleasers are not firm with their children, with those who work for them, or with anyone with whom they come into contact. They can't tell anyone else that they are displeased and can't say no to others' requests. As a result, they can in good faith make unrealistic commitments they are unable to fulfill.

People such as these try to avoid conflict at all costs and become upset when they can't comply with others' wishes. In order to avoid causing anger or displeasure, they refrain from taking the initiative or making decisions, fearing they might make the wrong choices.

People Pleasers are so accustomed to deferring to others that they have difficulty making decisions that involve themselves. They are so used to disregarding their own feelings that they often are not consciously aware of what they want. They have trouble differentiating between their own desires and those of their partners.

After a while, People Pleasers resent not getting their own needs met. They tend to choose (and are chosen by) those who insist on their own way most of the time, so resentments build up and lead to anger toward their mates. But out of fear they repress their anger, often covering it up with more compliance.

As a result, People Pleasers often find themselves depressed without knowing why. They recognize their difficulties in making decisions, they realize that they are not in control of their lives, and they feel upset and angry without fully understanding the cause.

It is likely that People Pleasers were not encouraged to make their own choices as children. They were probably criticized for expressing their opinions and told that decisions would be made for them. They were expected to do what their parents wanted. Either their parents were very strict and controlling or extremely critical—or both. In any case, the children's autonomy and sense of having the right to make their own choices were strongly discouraged. The children who tended to be compliant become People Pleasers, while the more rebellious children grow up angry and fearful of control by others.

Jimmy is a People Pleaser. His main goal, with his boss as well as his girlfriend, Anne, is not to make waves. At work he is known as a "yes man." Anne and everyone else who knows him thinks of Jimmy as a "really nice guy who would give you the shirt off his back." He has no enemies because he rarely makes an issue of anything and generally goes along with what others want.

Jimmy sounds like a perfect mate, yet Anne is unhappy with him. She says he never offers suggestions when they go out, and she complains that she has to do all the planning and make all the decisions about their future home. She feels that he doesn't care about anything.

Jimmy tries to please her by attempting to participate, but he is so unaccustomed to thinking about what he wants (except to please and not incur the wrath of those important to him), that he can't make choices. Anne becomes exasperated with him because she interprets this inability as a lack of caring about them and their home together.

Jimmy's other major fault is that he occasionally gets into black moods. Anne usually tries to be supportive, asking him to tell her what is wrong, but nothing seems to help. She fears that he is upset with her, but he will never say so. She says that she often wishes he would yell at her or refuse to do what she wants rather than get depressed.

THE MARTYR

The Martyr is an extreme case of People Pleaser. What makes her different is that she tolerates abuse from her mate. Although the People Pleaser submits to her mate's wishes, she is generally not mistreated since she usually chooses a mate who is a caretaker. He may be a Tyrant, a Mr. Macho, or a Workaholic, but he doesn't beat her, drink too much, or otherwise make her life miserable. The Martyr, on the other hand, chooses, and is chosen by, an abusive partner. While some Martyrs suffer in silence, most of them complain loudly about their sacrifices and what they "have to put up with." Their families, friends, and neighbors all commiserate with them about their mates' drinking, gambling, not working, philandering, or extravagant spending. They get a great deal of approbation and support from others by appealing to pity through their suffering and helplessness.

Although Martyrs suffer because of their mates' weaknesses and flaws, they often gain the upper hand by making their mates feel guilty. They constantly remind their spouses of how much pain or discomfort they undergo on their mates' behalf. For example, Martyrs might complain about how tired they are from staying up all night waiting for and worrying about their partners. They might lament having to wear "these old clothes" or "eating dinner alone night after night" because of the errant mates' gambling or drinking.

Martyrs have other advantages. They can get away with blaming their mates for many things and rarely have to look at their own shortcomings (since they are saints by comparison). When they complain too much and others ask, "Why do you put up with it?", they usually say, "Because he needs me," or "Because I love him." The truth is they can't leave—or change their way of functioning—because their self-esteem rests on being able to blame their partner for everything. Martyrs often feel that they are worthless and fear being without their mate. They suspect that nobody else would want them and so they have to "make the best of it." Martyrs appear to get nothing from their mates, but they are quite dependent on them.

Terry is known by all as a very good-hearted woman who has been handed a raw deal in life. She is married to Joe, who drinks too much, is often abusive, and has difficulty holding a job (in the last five years, he has lost three). According to Terry, he was always "let go" or "laid off" for reasons that had nothing to do with him. When he is working, Joe spends much of his salary on drinking—at bars with the boys or at home. Terry has to make do with very little money from him and pays for much of their household expenses out of her salary as a paraprofessional in an elementary school. Although he claims he loves her, Joe treats her badly. When he comes home from work, he demands a hot meal, no matter what kind of workday she has had. He doesn't help her clean up or do anything in the house because he is too tired from working all day. (Of course, she worked too, but that doesn't matter.) He is usually hypercritical, angry, and sharp with her. When he is slightly intoxicated, he orders her around like a slave. When he drinks a great deal, he becomes downright abusive, verbally and sometimes physically. He calls her vulgar names and pushes her around if she doesn't move fast enough or do things the way he wants them done.

When others ask her why she stays with Joe, Terry says she loves him. She says he would fall apart without her and that he can't help his drinking and his aggressive behavior when he drinks. She says that when he is sober he can be sweet and loving. Whenever she threatens to leave him, he promises to change and may stop drinking for a while. He tells her how much he needs her and how wonderful she is. He tells her how guilty he feels because she is "so good" and he is "so bad." Terry takes every opportunity to remind him of that.

It is difficult for others to understand Terry's behavior. She works, can support herself, and yet stays in a destructive relationship. What can she be gaining? Terry is very much afraid to be on her own. She needs to be with someone like Joe, who won't ever leave her because he can't. Also, Terry gets a great deal of support, sympathy, and admiration from her friends, colleagues, and family. She enjoys her reputation as a giving, loving saint. In the words of Robin Norwood, she is a "Woman Who Loves Too Much."

THE CLINGER

The Clinger is the classic overdependent person. Although usually female, Clingers can also be men, especially when they are older or sick.

Clingers look to their mates for incessant reassurance and emotional support. Frequently, they feel they are "stupid" no matter what their level of intelligence, and they see themselves as inadequate and unlovable. Consequently, they need their spouses to tell them over and over how much they love them and how wonderful they are. But since they rarely believe it, they require constant proof.

Because of their lack of confidence in themselves and in

their own judgment, Clingers can't make everyday decisions alone. They allow their spouses to decide such important matters as where they live, what kind of jobs they take, and with whom they socialize. Even when buying their clothes they need others' opinions. They generally refuse to go shopping alone and hate to take care of everyday chores by themselves.

Other IAs also have difficulties with decisions, but for different reasons. Whereas People Pleasers are afraid to displease their spouses and others, and consequently fear making the wrong decisions, Clingers feel incapable of making any decisions at all. People Pleasers are generally more capable than Clingers and frequently do too much for their mates (in order to please them); Clingers are generally overwhelmed by their jobs, chores, housework, or children.

Clingers go to great lengths to avoid being alone. If their partners go away on business trips or out with acquaintances, they will often stay with their families or friends. They will put up with a great deal of inconvenience to avoid spending time or doing things by themselves.

Clingers who are afraid to go out alone or stay alone can become agoraphobic. Agoraphobics are extremely fearful of being in public places, where they might become ill, upset, or anxious. They fear leaving their safe nest.

Many agoraphobics get "panic attacks" when they leave home, becoming so overwhelmed with severe anxiety that they feel they are going to die, become insane, or otherwise lose control. These attacks have all the physical symptoms of terror—shortness of breath, palpitations or accelerated heart rate, trembling, sweating, choking, nausea, chills or flushes, chest pain, faintness, or dizziness. Those who experience these attacks usually restrict their activities in order to avoid this tremendous anxiety. They fear the humiliation or embarrassment of agoraphobic symptoms as much as their physical discomfort.

Some agoraphobic Clingers do not go out of their homes at all, while others will go only to a few familiar places where they feel secure and comfortable—work, the supermarket, or the homes of close friends or family. Others will go places only when accompanied by their mates. These people are very dependent on their mates and greatly fear abandonment or even brief separation. They will often use their symptoms to get their mates to do their chores or to spend a great deal of time with them.

Because they feel so inadequate and dependent on others, many Clingers become depressed. They may also develop vague physical symptoms such as aches and pains that are not explainable by any illness. They may feel that they are too sick or too tired to take care of themselves. Some of them are hypochondriacs as well. Not only are they supersensitive to little aches and pains but they exaggerate their importance and interpret them as symptoms of major—even fatal—illness. These Clingers have difficulty functioning on their own because of the time and energy they spend resting or going to doctors.

Whether they are depressed, phobic, or merely extremely dependent, Clingers feel and act as if they need a great deal of help from their mates. Like other overdependent people, Clingers never developed enough autonomy and feelings of confidence in their abilities. Their parents discouraged them from growing and developing in a way that would enable them to become separate and independent.

Because they believe they can't manage by themselves, Clingers greatly fear abandonment. As a result, they will often subordinate themselves to their mates, so as not to be rejected. They seek and stimulate dominance and overprotectiveness in their partners. Ironically, their behavior may provoke the very rejection it was meant to protect against.

In their own way, however, Clingers are very demanding of their spouses, expecting them not only to do their own share but also to help with the Clingers' responsibilities. Clingers manipulate their partners through illness, fears, or incompetence. Spouses of such people, who may at first be gratified by being so needed, eventually may resent this situation.

Because Clingers feel so helpless and see their mates as so powerful, they can't see how exacting they are of their partners and how little they expect from themselves. They generally do not realize the extent of their impatience and their intolerance of others. If their spouses or lovers disappoint them in any way, by not calling or by coming late, for example, they may react with rage. They justify their anger, which is usually a reaction to their mate's lack of compliance with their wishes, by saying, and frequently believing, that their mate's behavior is evidence of lack of love.

When their mates show signs of weakness or human faults, Clingers are very threatened and may react with anger or fear. They are particularly lacking in understanding if their mates become ill. Instead of giving care and sympathy, they often become enraged and may accuse their partners of malingering to get attention. Ironically, they often accuse their spouses of being overdependent and childish.

Judy is a classic Clinger. She is a 35-year-old housewife with two children. She is very dependent on her husband for even the most minute decisions, such as what to make for dinner or what to wear to a party. She often complains about feeling overwhelmed by her responsibilities, even though the children spend most of their day at school and are reasonably well behaved at home. Since she is prone to migraine headaches and depressive moods, she needs much help with her chores and with the children. When she is menstruating, she becomes incapacitated, spending the first two days in bed.

Judy complains that her husband, Ron, doesn't spend enough time with her. She says he hardly ever tells her he loves her or buys her gifts. She wants him to call her at home at least twice a day. He usually does call her, but on those days when he is busy or forgets, she becomes hurt. When they were first married, Ron enjoyed catering to Judy. He felt strong and in control of the situation with her. She made him feel needed and gave him the confidence he needed to go out and conquer the world. However, after years of marriage, two children, and a business to run, he began to feel differently. He started to see Judy as a chain around his neck. He tries to help her but she becomes more and more incompetent and clinging as time goes on—and he becomes more resentful. He copes by spending more time at the office, which only makes her more frustrated and insecure.

THE TYRANT

Tyrants, whether male or female, are domineering and controlling of their mates. Male Tyrants may seem similar to Mr. Machos, who also dominate their mates, but Tyrants don't try to create the impression of being strong and capable. They don't act as if they can do everything for themselves. In fact, they admit they need their partners to take care of them. Like the Clinger, the Tyrant expects his mate to do a great deal for him, but he is more explicit and aggressive in his demands. His domineering and controlling manner serves to get his needs met while disguising his feelings of destitution. Unlike the Clinger, who manipulates through weakness or helplessness, the Tyrant manages his mate through coercive means (sometimes the same means other domineering IAs use).

The methods the Tyrant uses to get his way are determined by his personality, as well as by what works with his mate. Some Tyrants are very charming and can be gracious and fascinating when pleased. While obedience is rewarded liberally by these Tyrants, resistance is punished severely, sometimes with slashing attacks. They may resort to devices such as yelling and screaming when their mates don't comply with their wishes, and if that doesn't work, they may make a scene in public, knowing that their partners will do anything to avoid being socially embarrassed.

Like other IAs who might humiliate their partners, Tyrants were probably humiliated themselves in their childhood—by parents, siblings, other children, or teachers. Thus, they expect rebuke or humiliation from others and see it in their mates' refusal to give in to them.

Some Tyrants use character assassination or guilt slinging to win their points. They, like most people, are sensitive to their mates' vulnerabilities and play on them in order to manipulate a situation in their own favor. They don't usually respect off-limits topics and are known to hit below the belt when necessary to win.

Bringing the children in, either to provoke guilt or to induce the partner to give in to protect the children, is a common ploy of Tyrants.

Another widespread technique that Tyrants use is withholding love, affection, sex, or conversation. This may not be done explicitly; rather, the Tyrant feels "put off, tired, or upset" when he doesn't get his way, so how can he be responsive? Tyrants blame the lack of sex or affection on the spouse, saying, for example, "We fight, then you want sex." Whether sex or conversation is withheld will depend upon which one the partner wants more.

As a last resort, a few Tyrants use physical force. This is usually more of a male tactic, but some women, knowing their partners would feel guilty fighting back, have used it successfully.

Tyrants can't have an equal relationship. They are so needy and so fearful of being controlled that they fear if they aren't completely in charge, they will be frustrated. They don't consciously want to deprive their mates or take advantage of them, but their needs are so great that they can't tolerate any disappointments.

Gayle is a good example of a female Tyrant. Because she felt she needed a man to take care of her, she married Ray, a hardworking, silent man who acted as if he could handle everything. He was her "security blanket." Unlike Gayle, who was often hysterical, Ray was even-tempered and easygoing.

Although Gayle wanted to be taken care of, it had to be on her own terms. She insisted on making all the decisions and controlling everything that Ray did. If he didn't do her bidding, she would make his life miserable by screaming at him and withholding affection and sex. Since he was compliant by nature, he tended to become intimidated by her behavior and did what she asked.

She told him when he should work overtime and what he should do with his spare time. Although she didn't work, she insisted that he cook at least half the time and clean up most of the time. She acted as if she couldn't handle the slightest problem without his help—but demanded rather than asked for it.

Ray tried his best to please Gayle, but his income as a mechanic was not as much as Gayle would have liked. Since she felt unable to earn money herself, she nagged him for not providing enough. In response, he took on a second job, which resulted in his being tired in the evenings and having less time to help Gayle or to go out with her. She was chronically angry with him for letting her down.

THE COQUETTE

The Coquette is usually, but not always, a woman. She is openly affectionate and superficially devoted to her mate. Usually at-

tractive and lively, she can be very charming and appealing. She
also can exhibit an overdramatic quality that lacks genuineness.

Although this IA appears to be in love with her mate, she is
actually self-involved—overly invested in her appearance and in
getting her needs met instantly. She has no tolerance for frustration and overreacts to any minor inconvenience or obstacle to
getting what she wants.

She tends to be possessive and clingy, demanding a great
deal of attention and reassurance from her man. Like the Constant
Clinger, she acts as if she can't function on her own and needs
her lover desperately. However, unlike the Clinger, she is hardly
passive and quietly accepting. In fact, she is more similar to the
Tyrant in her desire to call the shots, though her style is different.
She may have tantrums, but they are often dramatic demonstra-
tions of need and love rather than angry outbursts such as the
Tyrant may have. She is likely to use her sexuality and seduc-
tiveness to get her way, and if that doesn't work, she may threaten
to hurt herself.

Another distinguishing characteristic of the Coquette is the
superficiality of her attachment to her lovers. The Constant Clinger and the Tyrant are basically very connected to and caring
about their mates, but the Coquette is closer to the Narcissist in
her lack of deep involvement. This becomes ap_ rent when, although she appears to be falling apart after a breakup, she perks
up amazingly quickly when she meets another attractive man or
when other men begin to pay attention to her.

Janet is a pretty 30-year-old woman. Very involved with her
physical appearance, she goes to the beauty salon every week and
the health spa practically every day, and shops a great deal. She
is vivacious and dramatic, becoming the center of attention wher-
ever she goes.

Janet has been seeing Bruce for about two years. She pro-
claims that she loves him so much she can't bear to be apart from
him and so she demands a great deal of his time and attention.
When he wants to watch TV or read, she becomes upset and says
he doesn't treat her as if he loves her. Bruce has to tell her constantly how beautiful and wonderful she is and how much he
loves her. In addition, her need for his hugging, kissing, and
touching seems unlimited.

When Janet has a fight with Bruce, she carries on as if the world were about to come to an end. She calls all her friends and family, Bruce's friends and family, and anyone else who will listen to her tale of woe. If he threatens to leave her, she threatens suicide. Since she once made a suicide gesture by taking a bottle of aspirins, Bruce takes her threats seriously and usually responds by giving in to her demands. However, he resents her manipulations and feels secretly angry with her, which further interferes with their intimacy.

THE PASSIVE PROCRASTINATOR

On the surface, the Passive Procrastinator looks like a People Pleaser because he seems agreeable and easy to get along with. His mate always seems to be in the wrong because he creates the impression of being so affable. It's hard to understand why she is often angry with him. She appears to be the "bitch."

The Passive Procrastinator goes along placidly with whatever his mate wants, but he usually doesn't follow through on his part. He never says he won't do something—help clean up, take out the garbage, or make those phone calls—but he delays. Later he merely forgets, falls asleep, or just can't find the time. It's never deliberate and it's never his fault.

The Passive Procrastinator rarely takes the initiative in relationships. He waits for his spouse to initiate affection, conversation, and sometimes sex. If she tries to involve him in cooperative planning, he can be exasperating. Like the People Pleaser, he can't reach a decision because he is afraid to displease and can't bear to disagree. So his mate might believe he is in agreement with her, although he isn't. She might later discover that he had no intention of following through on their "joint" plan.

Trying to discuss something or complain to this Intimacy Saboteur is equally frustrating. He refuses to fight and seems undisturbed when his partner is angry. When asked a direct question, he seems to ignore it. By being nonresponsive and not actively disputing his mate, he avoids her anger or disapproval. This noncommittal way of getting around issues is very common to this type of IA.

Why does the Passive Procrastinator act in such a frustrating, provocative way? He fears his wife's power and strength because he feels so dependent on her. As a result, he is afraid to confront her with his anger or disagreement. Yet, unlike the People Pleaser, he fears control too much to comply so he pretends to go along with and delays acting on their so-called joint decisions. He allows himself to be taken care of, and perhaps dominated, but ultimately gets even by resisting and denying.

Much of his behavior is entirely unconscious, serving to protect the Procrastinator from anxiety and conflict, but it can also be a calculated form of aggression. Many Passive Procrastinators are very much aware of the effects of their behavior on their spouses. As any partner of one of these IAs can attest, there is nothing more provocative than being ignored, or being led to believe that your partner agrees with you only to find that he won't follow through.

Passive Procrastinators are often sensitive people with a great deal of potential, education, and intelligence. However, they may not achieve up to their capabilities because of their passivity. When their mates try to encourage or pressure them, they are likely to become more and more resistant.

A variant of the Passive Procrastinator is his more aggressive cousin, The Defiant Disagreer, who actively resists any submission to his mate's requests. Instead, he gets angry and blames his partner for being too demanding.

Just as the People Pleaser feels she can't afford to say "no" to her mate, both the Defiant Disagreer and the Passive Procrastinator feel they can't afford to say "yes." They feel that their integrity demands that they not acquiesce. Similar to the rebellious teenager who feels that in order to be his own person he must defy his parents, they often act against their own best interests in the name of independence. If they were really independent, however, they would evaluate each situation on its own merits.

Behind the facade of defiance, these Intimacy Saboteurs are extremely dependent upon their mates, but they are threatened by this dependency. When their partners make them realize their own need to please, they become angry and resentful. They fear rejection and loss of approval, but they fear being controlled and manipulated more.

Dan is what everyone would describe as a "nice guy." He gets along with everyone and has no enemies. When he and his wife, Donna, get into a fight, even her friends and family believe that it is her fault. He appears so good to her that observers can't understand her frustration with him. However, when you speak to her, you get a very different picture of Dan. It's true that he never refuses her anything, but then he rarely performs what he promises. Unlike the People Pleasers whom he resembles, Dan doesn't really do whatever his wife wishes; he only pretends to go along with her to avoid any confrontation. When it is time to do what he agreed to do, he simply "forgets." He also seems to "forget" important appointments or birthdays and what Donna tells him she wants for her birthday.

Donna often gets exasperated with Dan for not doing what he promises. When she points this out to him, he refuses to reply, making matters worse. She wonders if he is being purposely hostile by clamming up and not responding to her as she becomes more and more angry.

Another complaint that Donna has about Dan is that he regularly falls asleep on the couch after dinner, especially evenings when they were planning to make love. She can't prove it, but she believes that he is punishing her for other things by limiting sex. Since he doesn't directly reject her but merely falls asleep, she has difficulty confronting him with her suspicions.

Dan is afraid of arguing with Donna about anything. He goes along, apparently agreeing with her views and plans. He doesn't consciously avoid doing what she wishes, he merely delays it. His general pattern is to put off until tomorrow whatever you don't want to deal with today. It enables him to get around many issues and maintain his image of "nice guy." Only when people know him better and have to depend upon him for things do they find him out as a Passive Procrastinator.

THE JEALOUS DOUBTER

The Jealous Doubter is very much afraid to trust her mate. But unlike other IAs who fear trusting and who defend against being hurt by distancing or not getting involved, she seeks connections. She is too dependent and needy to avoid close entanglements, so she becomes committed to someone and she worries. Will he be there for her when she needs him? Will he take advantage of her? Will he be unfaithful to her and humiliate her?

The Jealous Doubter suspects at the outset that her mate will betray her in one way or another. But since she loves him and needs him, she takes the chance, protecting herself and her interests the best she can by trying to control his activities or at least make him accountable for all his time. Jealous Doubters frequently get to know their mates' workplace. They may make friends with their husbands' secretaries or colleagues. They call frequently, ostensibly to chat but really to check up. By asking "innocent" questions they attempt to keep track of their spouses' whereabouts.

In order to feel secure, the Doubter demands complete exclusivity in her mate. She is jealous of his family, his friends, his work, his interests, and, often, their own children. She sees practically any activity that takes up his time or any interest or concern about others as a threat. Whenever he makes plans with others that don't include her, she becomes distraught and suspects infidelity. Since she easily feels left out and slighted, she is often angry with her spouse. Some Doubters have jealous rages; others become depressed and withdrawn. If her mate tries to reassure her, the Jealous Doubter doesn't believe him and so he can't appease her. Mates often feel frustrated, maligned, and angry because of the Doubters' constant suspiciousness and accusations.

Karen, a Jealous Doubter, is a 36-year-old married woman. Her husband, Bill, works overtime a great deal in order to pay the bills. Karen is very possessive toward him, always feeling that he prefers working or being with others to being with her. She is also very suspicious of Bill, continually fearing that he is cheating on her.

Bill complains that Karen is so jealous of his time that she doesn't allow him the freedom to see his friends or stay after work for a drink with his coworkers. In order to avoid confrontation with her, he has lied to her on numerous occasions, telling her he was working when he really was with friends.

Several times she discovered his lies by checking up on him at work. When confronted, he said her oversuspicious behavior causes him to feel "locked in." He feels he has to lie to her just to get time to see friends. Regardless of what he says, she is afraid of trusting him. Has she any concrete reason? She says, "No, but all men are like that—you can't trust any of them."

When Karen was a child, her mother confided in her about problems she was having with Karen's father. Because of her mother's distrust of men, Karen learned to distrust men also. Through her constant possessiveness and suspiciousness, Karen subtly encourages her husband to lie in his own defense. Although making matters worse by lying, he feels unable to deal with his wife's anger and control any other way. Her expectations for loyalty are unrealistic; so she is continually disappointed. She interprets her husband's behavior as disloyalty to her, which increases her suspiciousness of him. He feels more and more controlled by the situation and reacts by withdrawing from her.

THE MOST INDIRECT of the IAs are the Intimacy Saboteurs. Instead of appearing to shrink from closeness, they seem to embrace it. They want togetherness with their partners, but on their terms. Each type, in its own way, places demands on mates that frequently cause them to withdraw in self-defense.

The Constant Critic and the Jealous Doubter push their mates away with criticism and endless scrutiny. The Sulker, the Clinger, the Coquette, and the Tyrant are too dependent and needy for most people's comfort. While the Sulker and Clinger whine about their needs, the Tyrant demands that his be met. The Passive Procrastinator can be infuriating in his apparently innocent, well-meaning manner of saying "yes" but not following through. People Pleasers and Martyrs, although creating the impression of being easier to live with, also exact a price, usually paid in guilt, and they are frequently resentful of their mates and let them know it.

Intimacy Saboteurs are also subject to the same fears of closeness that haunt Distancers and Pseudo-Intimates. What distinguishes them are their strong dependency needs, which override their fears and cause them to cling rather than retreat.

5

The Compromisers—
Partners of IAs

Who are the partners of IAs? What are they like, those people who are attracted to—and remain in relationships with— IAs? Many of them are Intimacy Avoiders themselves. While appearing to seek true intimacy, they want to regulate it, and tailor-make it, so that they feel comfortable. They look, unconsciously, for someone to meet their "neurotic" needs for a limited intimacy. They feel safer connected to someone who puts up barriers to intimacy and who is satisfied with less closeness than with someone who wants more.

These people frequently can't admit their own need for distance. By getting involved with an IA, they can believe they have a good relationship without having to overcome their own difficulties with closeness. If they become aware that their relationship is lacking, they can always blame their partner rather than recognize their own contribution to the situation.

Couples often "fit" in terms of their mutual need for less than intimate relationships. They might "hook into each other" and participate in an unconscious contract that meets the needs of both and hurts neither. For example, those who need to be in control will seek mates who like to please or are afraid to displease. Those who fear abandonment will tend to look for partners who give them constant reassurance and won't ever leave them (perhaps because of their own fears or dependencies).

Unfortunately, however, these relationships are often tenuous ones that wind up leading to more and more compromises and unhappiness. They are based on weakness, fears, and over-dependencies, and if either partner grows or changes the balance shifts and resentments and dissatisfactions develop. (This has begun to happen in many modern relationships, as women are becoming stronger and more independent. They are no longer willing to accept their husbands' domination or emotional distance.)

EMOTIONAL COMPROMISES

Certain combinations of IAs are particularly common. For example, two Distancers or Pseudo-Intimates can often marry and be comfortable with each other, because neither expects too much. Their marriage may even appear ideal to others. They can both be independent and yet share a home, children, friends, and interests. They are usually very congenial, and seldom argue. The only catch is they are emotionally distant. You can see this in the case of the two Status Seekers described in Chapter 3.

Controlling woman and Passive Procrastinator In some cases it is difficult to say which of the two partners in a relationship is more of an IA. Speaking to either one of them will lead you to believe that it is the other partner who is at fault and that the complainant is merely reacting to a difficult situation.

Take the relationship of Barry and June, for example. Barry, a 30-year-old businessman, is involved with June, a woman he finds very exciting. He describes her as "attractive, bright, and scintillating." Barry is generally happy with June, but often finds her too demanding. For example, she always expects to eat at either her favorite health food restaurant or her favorite Japanese restaurant, and she insists that they always sleep at her house rather than occasionally staying at his. This puts him in a bind. He feels pressured to conform to her demands, afraid that she might leave him, but very angry to be "over a barrel." While at first he tried to please her, as he felt more sure of her he became more and more resentful and more unwilling to comply. Now he stubbornly resists whatever she suggests. He says that every time she expresses her preferences he feels himself hardening. He feels that he has to "watch out or she'll plow right over me, and my needs." She is becoming more and more demanding and complains that he won't do anything she wants, even when her wishes are reasonable.

Why did Barry and June get into this type of destructive interaction? Barry is a dependent man who hides his neediness under a cloak of competence. Although he is an effective businessman, quite capable of taking care of himself and others in practical matters, he needs a great deal of emotional support and reassurance from his mate. June can give him this—but at a price. She wants her own way. If Barry were merely dependent and needy, he might comply. But he also fears control. He is afraid to comply, and he is afraid to recognize his own need for support and nurturance. When June becomes demanding, he feels so pressured that he immediately becomes angry and resentful of finding himself in such a dependent position. He feels that he has to say no to maintain his own self-respect and integrity.

Dependent woman and controlling man   A dependent, needy woman who is willing to trade control for being taken care of often marries a man who needs to be in control all the time. He is willing to take on more responsibility and work in order to be in charge, and in return gets his wife's admiration and affection. As long as he is willing and able to take care of both of them, the situation can remain stable.

However, these relationships are bound to fail at some point because the attraction is based on weakness, not strength. Secure, emotionally independent people generally do not need to prove themselves by taking on the burden of an overdependent partner, whereas more needy people might. Since the men who enter into these relationships are not as strong as they appear to be, they can't sustain for long the burden of their more dependent mate. Or, the woman might become stronger and want more power in the relationship, which could also lead to failure of this type of emotional pairing. This is what happened with Arthur and Barbara.

Arthur is a physician working with a medical group. Barbara is a housewife. They have two children. When the children were young, Barbara stayed home to raise them. Arthur made all the major decisions about how they were to spend their money, where they lived, and what they did with their leisure time. After a number of years, the children went to school. Barbara spent her time redoing the house and herself at great expense. Arthur still took care of all the family's financial obligations and made all of the decisions.

Until that point they appeared to be doing fine. Suddenly, Arthur became seriously depressed. He began to feel overwhelmed and unable to handle things, and he became extremely worried about money. Although he earned a very respectable income, they were deeply in debt, largely because of Barbara's spending.

Arthur had mixed feelings about his situation. On one hand, he felt like a failure, unable to adequately provide for his family, and he began to doubt his ability as a doctor. On the other hand, he was enraged at Barbara for her extravagance and for not getting a job to help pay the bills. Even so, on the latter issue, Arthur was ambivalent. Since he was raised to believe that a man should support his family totally, Barbara's earning money would be further proof of his failure. Yet, while he liked the feeling of being in charge and making all the decisions, he did not like having to bear the total financial burden, especially when expenses rose. Because of his conflicted feelings, he was either enraged or depressed.

From Barbara's viewpoint, Arthur was there to provide what she wanted for herself and for her children. That had been their unspoken agreement. When he became tight with money because of his fears, she became angry. He was not fulfilling his promise to take care of her. If there wasn't enough money for what she thought they needed, then he should make more.

Arthur's depression became serious enough to interfere with his work. Although he had previously seen himself as self sufficient and too strong to need anyone's help, when the situation became desperate and the other doctors recommended therapy he reluctantly agreed. In therapy, he began to see that his tremendous facade of overindependence was covering his fear of being too needy. His belief that he was totally in control of things at home was not really accurate; while he made a show of making the decisions himself, he was very much influenced by his need to impress others, including his wife and children. His feelings about himself required that he provide for his family in a certain style and that he allow his wife free rein in spending money. He saw that his wife's opinion was too important to him, and that, in general, his need to impress others with his strength and power made him vulnerable to their manipulation. This caused him problems, the least of which was his current financial bind. He could not get himself out of his difficulties because he could not admit that he was not invincible—that he needed his wife's support, emotionally and financially. He could no longer treat her like a pampered child; it had become too much of a burden and was causing him deep resentment that surfaced as criticisms and outbursts of rage at her for trivial things.

Barbara also began therapy, ostensibly for support in dealing with her husband. As therapy progressed she began to examine why she was so enraged with him. She explored her overdependency and came to realize that in spite of all of her excuses, the real issue was that she did not want to get a job and that she resented even the suggestion of it by Arthur or anyone else. She did not even want to see the bills, much less help pay them or in any way deal with the consequences of her own spending. Basically, she wanted to be taken care of and was extremely angry that suddenly Arthur was changing the rules.

The exploration in therapy revealed that she was afraid of getting a job because she was convinced that her contributing to her own support would prove that she wasn't as good as the other women in her neighborhood who could stay home. She also was afraid that she was not proficient or talented enough to get and hold a good job.

Because of their strong feelings and fears, Arthur and Barbara avoided adopting a budget or attempting to cut down on expenses. They could legitimately blame each other without having to look at themselves. They continued to be angry and resentful while feeling inadequate in themselves.

After some work in therapy they both were more ready to cooperate. At first Arthur resisted any attempt by his wife to assume responsibility and gain some control. However, with support and understanding his attitude began to change. These people still have much to work out, but they are talking and negotiating. By changing the way they see themselves both will win.

Controlling woman and dependent man Another common two-IA situation involves a dependent People Pleaser who hides his dependency by marrying a controlling but needy woman. On the surface he takes care of her, but she tells him what to do. She calls all the shots while he passively acquiesces. Somewhere along the way, however, she might get angry with him for not taking charge of things.

Charles was a hardworking, solid, and easygoing guy. He looked as if he could deal with anything. He married Jill when they were both in their early twenties. They have two children. Jill appeared sweet and agreeable when they first met, but soon after their wedding she showed herself to be a Tyrant. Charles never said no to whatever she wanted. In fact, Charles was not as strong and independent as he might have appeared. He was afraid to assert his needs because of his own dependency. His mother was an extremely controlling woman who would withhold love when she was not heeded. Charles had been a compliant child who grew up to be a compliant adult—a People Pleaser.

After an initial period of calm in their marriage, Charles and Jill began to have problems. He could no longer continue to please her; she wanted control without responsibility. Because of his fear of Jill's criticism and rejection, Charles allowed her to control everything, but neither partner was taking responsibility. Consequently they got into debt, and Jill blamed Charles.

He became resentful, but kept it buried deeply. He never complained. Instead he got fat, stopped taking care of himself, and spent a good deal of the time asleep on the couch. Part of his response was due to depression and feelings of inadequacy. The rest was passive aggressive behavior. He could not respond directly to Jill for fear of her anger, so he passively withdrew from her.

Jill and Charles came to therapy to save their marriage. After some time, Jill began to understand why she had married a man whom she felt would take care of her but whom she could control. After a while, she was able to take some of the responsibility for their financial situation. She could see that she might have been more involved all along and not left everything to Charles. He acted as if he were in complete control of things but he wasn't because he was afraid of her. She got a part-time job at first, and when her youngest child went to school she began working full-time. She gradually assumed more of the budgeting responsibilities. Neither one of these people is good at planning or postponing what they want, but at least they are working together for the first time. Charles also has become a bit more assertive, first at work, then with his mother, and now with Jill. While at first she resented his assertiveness with her, Jill has accepted it as a necessary part of Charles's growth.

Stable man with "neurotic" woman   Sometimes an apparently stable, healthy man gets involved with a very disturbed, difficult woman. What makes a reasonable, responsible person exercise such poor judgement in choosing a mate? Some people who marry dependent, neurotic people who cannot function by themselves do so to avoid intimacy. They see themselves as good, caring people who want more closeness but can't get it because their spouses are "sick." If the spouses were to become better, they would then have to face their own fears of closeness.

If one of the partners is weak and ineffectual but not destructive, the couple might appear to have a good marriage without risking too much intimacy. At times, however, the neurotic spouse becomes a tyrant, controlling the relationship and the other person by making constant demands.

Alan was a divorced man in his late 30s who met and fell in love with a much younger woman. Linda was attractive and vivacious and made him feel young and vital. Alan was very stable—even stodgy—and responsible. He worked hard and was careful about money. On the other hand, Linda was flamboyant, exciting, and a little irresponsible. While she didn't always live up to his standards for homemaking or keeping appointments, she made up for it with enthusiasm and effervescence.

As their relationship developed, it became clear that Alan couldn't count on Linda for many things. Soon after they began living together, she quit her job, saying she couldn't get along with her co-workers. She became very demanding and unreasonable at home, for example, expecting him to build an elevator between the first floor and the basement. If she was thwarted in any of her desires she had a tantrum—at home or anywhere. Her anger frightened Alan and made him give in to her. He talked about leaving her, but always said he couldn't: what would she do without him?

Then things would calm down and Linda would be "wonderful." When things went her way, Linda was in good spirits and was great fun to be with. She and Alan laughed a lot, played more than ever, and had passionate sex. She seemed to enjoy life and he enjoyed sharing life with her.

Alan hated living on a seesaw but felt unable and unwilling to leave Linda. Why was he so attached to her?

He was attracted to the alive feeling he got, being with a woman who was more childlike and less inhibited than he. He could identify with her freedom from controls and her self-indulgence, and revel in them. He was generally quiet, inhibited, responsible, hard-working, and serious about life. She was playful, lived for the moment, and wanted immediate gratification. He couldn't be like her but found her exciting and refreshing to be around.

Alan and men like him work hard and become overresponsible to compensate for feelings of inadequacy. This is why they feel they have to do well in their business or profession. They often don't feel comfortable socially—dating or going out with friends. The women who attract them are often uninhibited socially and will actively chase them. These men are usually flattered that an attractive woman is interested in them and relieved that they don't have to do the pursuing.

Taking care of a needy woman builds this type's ego. He feels important and proud that she needs him so much, and he doesn't have to worry about losing her as he might if she were more independent.

His self-esteem is inflated further since he is so much better than she is, in so many ways. In this he is like the Martyr. He can always complain about her and never have to deal with his own shortcomings, especially since, in contrast to his mate, he is so very responsible and rational.

WHY OTHERS CHOOSE INTIMACY AVOIDERS

A great many people who are not themselves IAs become involved with mates who evade closeness. How do they choose IAs, and why do they stay with them? Obviously choosing an IA satisfies some strong need.

One of the major reasons that many people choose intimacy avoiders is their upbringing. It is a commonly held belief among family therapists that you cannot have a better marriage than your parents did. While this maxim isn't entirely true, there is some validity to it. Everyone's first ideas about relationships originate by witnessing his or her parents.

By observing their mothers and fathers, children learn about men and women and what to expect from each of them. As the children mature they gradually formulate attitudes and feelings toward both sexes. Whether they like, respect, and trust others, or fear and hate them, develops from these early experiences.

Melanie Klein and other object-relations theorists (who built on and expanded Freudian concepts of psychoanalytic theory) see human personality development as determined by the infant's crucial experiences with his or her primary caretakers. This is the prototypic intimate relationship. They believe that we all have images in our minds (Melanie Klein called these "imagos") that represent people and relationships from our early experiences. (The word "object" in object-relations theory refers to a love object; "object relations" means the emotional attachment between the person who loves and the internalized mental image of the loved one.)

Many studies bear this theory out. They indicate that women have greater problems forming lasting relationships if during their childhood their fathers were uninvolved, ineffective, or hostile. Their desire to get married and have children and even their sexual responsiveness and satisfaction were found to be related to an affectionate, attentive, supportive relationship with their fathers.

What a youngster anticipates of intimate involvements also develops by watching his parents. The quality of his parents' interactions with each other and with him—loving and supportive, hostile and critical, or mixed—is what he presumes is natural. It becomes his unconscious scenario of male–female relationships and the nature of marriage. When he gets involved or marries, these images surface.

Dr. Carl Hindy of the University of North Florida and Conrad Schwarz of the University of Connecticut studied the connection between a person's love life and past relationships with parents. They found that the image of the parent of the opposite sex was crucial. For example, men who were overinvested in lovers, complaining that their affection wasn't returned, generally had mothers who were unapproachable and relatively uninvolved with them. Women who were overanxious about their attachments had fathers who were detached or hostile.

Psychoanalysts and family therapists believe we try to recreate our childhood relationships with our opposite-sex parent in our current involvements. Many do this, whether deliberately or without awareness, by marrying spouses who remind them of their first heterosexual love—their mother or father. The spouses' traits are familiar and revive old feelings from childhood. Because our opposite-sex parents were our first loves, when we were most impressionable, many of their traits become highly valued. So we tend to be attracted to mates who are similar in personality or in other significant ways. When people get involved with mates such as these, they are unconsciously maintaining ties with their parents.

Others marry men or women different from their parents, but still attempt to recreate the old well-known relationship. They react to their spouses as they learned to react to their parents and they expect from them what they repeatedly experienced from their parents. Even without conscious awareness, these indelibly etched scenarios are played out.

For example, Iris has always been treated like a "princess" by her father. As a result, she dates only men who are warm and giving toward her. She says, "Why should I put up with not being treated well?"

Unlike Iris, Ginny never seems to meet men who are considerate. She says, "All the men I get involved with spend too much time with their friends and never want to go anywhere. They are all deadheads, just like my father."

Women who as children lost fathers because of death or

divorce are even more likely than other women to look for a father-replacement in their husbands. But because they have only their childhood images of their fathers, the men they marry are often more similar to these images than to the real thing. Studies have shown that women whose fathers have died tend to idealize their memories of them, while women from divorced homes view their fathers as worse than other men in general. This is most likely a reflection of their mothers' attitudes.

Why You Might Desire Someone Similar to an Ungratifying Parent

It is understandable that people tend to love mates who share their fathers' or mothers' strengths or who treat them as well as their parents did. But what happens if their parents were not all of these things—if their parents were distant, cold, or even destructive? Most might deliberately avoid people who are like that. However, many people, in spite of their conscious desire to find a different kind of mate, find themselves involved with one similar to their unsatisfying parents. Although each person's reasons are different, several patterns emerge.

Expectations because of early experience   Just as people can learn to expect warmth and love from their mates because of good early relationships, they can learn to expect less than positive interactions if their early relationships were poor. We feel more at ease with mates who treat us as we are used to being treated because we have developed ways to deal with them. Other types might make us feel uncomfortable because we wouldn't know how to deal with them or what to expect.

For example, Nancy explains, "My father was very strict with me and my sister—and very bossy with my mother. Although I was afraid of his anger, I always felt secure knowing that he would take care of everything. I never learned to make decisions for myself, so I was naturally attracted to someone like David, who also took total charge. But after we were married a while, I found that I didn't like being treated like a child."

Nancy learned from early experiences to expect men to be in charge and somewhat condescending to women. She also learned from her father, and her mother, that women defer to men. Her marriage followed the same pattern as that of her parents. However, as she began to grow, she resented her husband's behavior and wanted to assume more responsibility in the relationship. She blamed her husband for being too controlling, never recognizing that she chose him in part because of this quality.

Belief it is their own fault   Children tend to blame themselves for their parents' injustices. Because they are so dependent upon their parents, they would rather see themselves as imperfect than attribute blame to their caretakers. When they get involved or marry, and their partners treat them badly, as their parents did, they expect it (as described above) and blame themselves.

They feel that if they were different they would be loved more or given more. Children are very much aware of their weaknesses and "bad feelings." They know how angry, greedy, selfish, and sexual they can feel. Since they often don't live up to their parents' and their own internalized standards, they believe that their parents' behavior is due to their own transgressions.

Frank blamed himself for his wife's constant flirting with other men. He said "She's so young and attractive and loves to have a good time. I'm always working and never take her anywhere. No wonder she looks at other men. But I worry that she might leave me. You can't trust women, they're all alike."

When Frank's mother ignored him and preferred his brother when he was a child, he believed that it was his fault—that he wasn't good or lovable enough. He internalized those feelings and continued to blame himself for things like his wife's flirting when he became an adult.

Wish to reform partner   Men and women who love mates with destructive traits like those of their parents usually want to help them. In this they are often trying to recreate their childhood. As children, they may have been the only ones who understood their parents. More often, they felt inadequate because they couldn't make their parents "better" or different.

Since children need their parents to take care of them, they are very much invested in their parents' emotional strength. As a result, when parents have problems, the children usually want to heal them. They frequently believe their parents' problems are their fault, which makes them feel even more responsible.

When these children become adults, they pursue opportunities to try again by helping others like their parents. In this way, they can rectify, on an unconscious level, their unsatisfying relationships with their parents.

Sharon found herself in love with a man who drank too much, in spite of her hatred of her father's drinking. She explained, "I can't stop loving him just because he drinks. He's unhappy and my love can help him give up drinking. Sure, I find him funny and exciting when he drinks—he's totally uninhibited and does wild things. But that's not why I love him." She is unaware that part of her attraction to this man is his similarity to her father. Through him, she hopes to do what she couldn't as a child—reform the man she loves.

When Do People Look for a Different Kind of Mate?

Sometimes a person seeks a mate who is very different from a destructive opposite-sex parent. If there were positive experiences with others, such as the other parent, a grandparent, or another relative or friend, this person may overcome a tendency to be attracted to destructive mates.

Gina says, "I vowed never to marry a man like my father. After hearing my mother's complaints all my life, I was turned off to passive men." Her husband, Don, is very ambitious and outgoing.

How did Gina overcome the tendency to be attracted to men who resembled her father? How did she avoid the trap of blaming herself, or trying to reform her mate, or learning to expect such behavior from all men? The major reason is that she had a positive relationship with a strong, nurturing mother.

When women have highly responsive mothers whom they feel they can trust, they tend to look for husbands with qualities similar to their mothers'. Psychologist Arthur Aron and his colleagues interviewed 46 males and 52 females who were about to get married. They found that, with regard to important aspects of relationships, both men and women often seek to repeat in their marriage the relationship they had with their mother. For women, there were significant similarities between their future spouses and their mothers in the areas of responsiveness and trust.

Donna's father was very self-involved and inconsiderate. When she was growing up, Donna felt that her mother sacrificed herself for her father. On the other hand, Donna's aunt and uncle had a much more loving relationship. In addition, her uncle was very fond of Donna and spent a great deal of time reading to her and taking her fishing. When she became a young woman, Donna consciously looked for a man similar to her uncle rather than her father. Although she loved her father, she didn't want to be married to someone like him.

Even without positive experiences with opposite-sex models who are different from a hurtful parent, someone may decide to avoid a mate similar to that parent. Many men and women look for mates who provide the stability, affection, or even distance (if their parents were too intrusive) they couldn't get from their parents. Some men will consider getting involved only with women who, unlike their clingy dependent mothers, are very self-sufficient. Women whose fathers disappointed them and their mothers by not earning enough, frequently require that their partners be financially successful. This works out well except when carried to extreme, as, for example, when avoiding mates similar to a parent causes someone to reject practically all potential mates. For example, Mel, in Chapter 2, consistently avoided women who were the slightest bit controlling because his mother had been so over-controlling. As a result, he never allowed himself to become attached to anyone.

Another way in which people can overcome their tendency to become attached to the wrong partners is by becoming aware of their patterns of attraction and the reasons for them. When they see that they are continually getting involved with IAs of a certain type, they can analyze why. By recognizing that their potential mates revive childhood feelings rather than satisfy adult needs, they have a better chance of avoiding these unfortunate attachments.

Cindy, a woman who is involved with an Affair Seeker, said, "I never realized it, but Jim reminds me so much of my father. When I was a child, I didn't believe my mother when she accused my father of cheating—but now I think he did." After examining the reasons for her attraction to Jim, Cindy decided to avoid the pain of continuing her involvement with him. Although choosing to believe that Jim would have left his wife to marry her, she still thought it best to end the affair. "Even if he does marry me," she said, "I'll never quite trust him. I couldn't take the insecurity." Cindy was lucky; she had developed enough self-esteem to be able to let go of a destructive relationship.

~~~~~

THIS CHAPTER has described the emotional compromises many people make when they get involved with IAs. Some of these people are IAs themselves and, until they solve the problems that cause them to shun closeness, need to relate to others who similarly limit intimacy. They generally find others with whom they fit in terms of "neurotic" needs. I have described several typical IA combinations in the beginning of the chapter.

Others who choose IAs do so because the IAs remind them of beloved parents. These people are driven to rework their childhood relationships in their current ones.

As adults, we have many role models besides our parents. We have the opportunity to observe many types of relationships and can choose the one that meets our needs. The first step is to identify how we are currently relating. Then we need to understand the reasons behind our behavior.

In the chapters that follow, you will learn the underlying causes for avoidance of intimacy in all its forms, including the choice of an IA as a mate. Then you can begin to overcome these forces.

The Veils Between Us

How People Become Intimacy Avoiders

6

Trust

Trust is the cornerstone of a relationship. Without it there can be no true intimacy. Yet trust is one of most difficult things to establish between people. Why is it so hard to trust someone else?

There are three major aspects of trust—predictability, dependability, and faith.

When we place trust in others, the first thing we expect is that they will be predictable. We need to know that our mates will behave in a consistent manner. If they change moods unpredictably or react to our behavior in different ways at different times, we won't know what to expect from them.

Dependability in our mates is also of utmost importance. Mates should be available to us when we need them, and not let us down or abandon us. Partners should never deliberately harm us. We expect them not to betray our secrets to others or use our confidences to gain an advantage over us. Furthermore, we hope they won't humiliate or embarrass us, or be overly harsh and critical. When we are disappointed with others or ourselves, and when we feel hurt or rejected by others, we trust our partners to be supportive and understanding.

Faith is the last aspect of trust. The other aspects of trust can be observed; faith is based on expectations of future behavior.

We want the security of our mates' continuing responsiveness and caring in the future—even if present circumstances change.

While most of us, although cautious at first, eventually begin to trust our partners more and more, IAs remain generally reluctant to trust. All IAs exhibit some lack of trust in their mates, but most of them have a basic sense of trust in their partners and their fears are confined to one or two areas. These fears are usually manageable enough to allow some modicum of closeness in their relationships.

Extreme IAs—whether Distancers, Pseudo-Intimates, or Intimacy Saboteurs—usually show a great lack of trust. Many of them are afraid to trust anyone. Their experience of getting close to another is fraught with danger—the danger of being submerged or swallowed up, controlled, rejected, or used and abandoned. For them, the risk is too great. They are too fearful of being hurt to allow themselves to really trust.

IAs who strongly fear trusting are usually extreme Distancers such as Loners, Perfectionists, or Romanticists who avoid commitment completely. Pseudo-Intimates and Intimacy Saboteurs who have problems with trust usually erect elaborate defenses that prevent them from placing more than the minimum faith and trust in their mates.

HOW FEAR OF TRUSTING AFFECTS INTIMACY

People who fear trusting either avoid close relationships or regulate the distance in their relationships so that they feel safe. Suspecting that others will take advantage of them and not give to them, they attempt to protect themselves and preserve their interests by always making sure they get their share of everything —food, sex, money, or favors. For example, they might check to see that they get the largest slice of meat or pie when food is being divided, or that they never pay more than their share of the bill when they eat out with others. And they always keep track of whose turn it is to do the dishes or other chores.

Many IAs say they are reluctant to trust in a new relationship because they have been burnt by others in the past. Although this can be an excuse to cover their real fears, it may very well be true. People having problems with trust also have needs for closeness. Because of their lack of experience in relationships, they rarely develop good judgment about people. They do not know how to determine whether others are trustworthy or capable of fulfilling their particular needs or requirements, which leads to occasions when they trust others too much or when they trust the wrong people. Then they are hurt and become afraid to trust again.

Some IAs try to guard against being hurt by limiting their emotional investment in their partners. When they care for others, they avoid letting them know. Or they may try to protect themselves by avoiding self-disclosure, which they fear their partners could use against them.

These people are extremely sensitive to what they perceive as betrayals of trust. If their partners break implicit pacts with them (even if their partners are not aware of the pacts) or if their partners break promises, no matter what the circumstances, they feel betrayed. Since they readily feel exposed to others, they are stringent about what they consider confidences. If their partners should innocently repeat what was confided as a secret, even if it was an insignificant remark, IAs interpret this as a violation of trust.

To allay their deep fears of being unlovable and therefore unloved by their mates, people such as these often require their would-be partners to give guarantees of almost unconditional acceptance. They want constant proof that they are loved and that they will be accepted no matter how they behave. They unrealistically expect their mates not to criticize them, or get angry with them, or leave them for any reason. Often they also expect that others will always give them what they want—even forgoing their own wishes to do so. Their unconscious assumption is that their partners are there to fulfill their needs. (This is not usually consciously acknowledged, but it is nonetheless acted upon.) Anything their partners may gain from their relationship is seen by IAs as instant proof that their mates are merely using them. Since others can never fulfill these requirements and satisfy their insatiable and impossible demands, the IAs' convictions of being unloved are confirmed.

Another condition that these very insecure people place on their lovers is that of complete exclusivity. They are pathologically jealous of those who might take their lovers' attention for even a moment. Any affection that must be shared with a friend, child, or parent is devalued. They are suspicious of their mates' relationships with others and are constantly on guard against their mates' betraying them with another lover. When there is a realistic threat to a valued relationship, jealousy is perfectly normal and generally accepted. However, if someone is continually jealous and suspicious, in the absence of any evidence of betrayal, there is a real problem of trust. Since even the most loyal mates cannot dispel their suspicions or meet their expectations for any length of time, these IAs become further convinced that their partners are untrustworthy.

People who fear trusting others often cause their own worst fears to come true. Because they anticipate being taken advantage of or betrayed, they treat others with suspicion. They are easily convinced that others are letting them down and as a result feel very angry with them much of the time. In addition, because they feel they have to protect themselves they become greedy and ungiving, thereby causing others to withdraw from them. They never take the risk of giving first, sharing with others, or allowing themselves to care for others. They sabotage the development of intimacy that would enable them to trust their partners. In this way, they fulfill their own prophecy that others cannot be trusted.

Fear of trusting can take many forms and leads to many different types of behavior. For some, like Karen, described in the section on the Jealous Doubter, the main fear is their mates' sexual infidelity. However, for most who fear trusting, the suspicions of being betrayed are much more general.

Jean is an example of a woman who lacks basic trust. She tearfully expresses the feeling that she is "all alone in the world and cannot count on anyone else." Her fiancé, Dan, is devoted to his mother and sister and she doesn't feel included in this inner circle. Believing that Dan places his mother and sister first, before her, makes Jean very resentful. She is afraid that if she ever needs him in an emergency, he will not come through for her. Because of her fears, she expects unreasonable proof from him that he will not let her down. She is constantly pitting herself against his mother to see if he will pass the test and choose her. This places

Dan in an impossible situation. He cannot go against his mother, who is elderly, widowed, and helpless in his eyes, and he doesn't want his fiancée to be hurt and angry with him. Neither of them can win in this situation. Jean always sees him choose his mother, and when she confronts him, he accuses her of being jealous—and he is right. Jean is frightened of trusting. She does not expect anyone to come through for her and sees her fiancé's loyalty to his family as proof positive that she will never be able to count on him. By setting up the situation in which he has to choose, she is making it impossible for Dan to reassure her.

Extreme Problems with Trust

A few IAs have such extreme problems with trust that they may be considered almost paranoid. These people feel so vulnerable that they fear everyone is against them. They are constantly enraged at others because they feel used and deprived.

Often these people defend against their feelings of vulnerability and deprivation by aggressively seeking power and control over others. To protect themselves from feeling bad about their rage and their wishes for control and power, they project these feelings onto others—that is, they deny having the feelings themselves and instead attribute them to someone else. This is an unconscious and automatic defense mechanism. People who use projection as a defense aren't conscious of their own aggressive wishes. They truly believe that others are being hostile toward them. As a result, they feel even more vulnerable and in need of self-defense and interpret their aggressive behavior toward others as self-protection rather than attack.

Sometimes projection makes people unrealistically suspicious of their mates' sexual infidelities. For example, if they are or have been sexually unfaithful, or if they would like to be unfaithful, they are likely to suspect their spouses of infidelity. This has long been observed by psychotherapists and has recently been confirmed by research. A survey on jealousy for *Psychology Today* done by psychologists Peter Salovey and Judith Rodin shows that those who report having had affairs while in committed relationships are more likely to be suspicious of their mates.

WHY ARE PEOPLE AFRAID TO TRUST?

They have been hurt by parents whom they couldn't trust.
Erik Erikson, a developmental psychoanalyst who based his work on Freud, described the basic stages of personality development. The major task of the first two years of life is the development of what he called "basic trust." If parents meet their children's needs in a reasonably consistent way, without causing undue frustration, the children develop a sense of "basic trust" in others. They will have a generally positive expectation that others will meet their needs.

Those who develop fears of trusting were let down by their parents in their very early childhood. Their parents were usually psychologically unavailable because of alcoholism, drug addiction, mental illness, or severe emotional difficulties, and so they were too involved with their own needs to respond consistently to their infant's needs even in the most basic ways. These infants were subject to great neglect and frustration and were traumatized as a result. Understandably they grew up feeling untrusting of others. They don't expect anyone to care about them or do anything for them. They expect others to disappoint them as their parents did.

A child who is continually frustrated by his parents usually blames himself. Such a child believes his parents did not love him—not because of his parents' flaws or problems, but because he was unworthy or bad. When he becomes an adult, he still feels that he is not deserving of love from others, which strengthens his conviction that he cannot depend on others.

They were less favored than their siblings.
Children who have developed "basic trust" may still be suspicious of those they love; that is, they may have a general sense of trust toward newcomers, friends, and even strangers, but may fear that their loved ones won't continue to love them. This feeling can come about if their parents seem to prefer their siblings to them, or if they feel neglected after the birth of younger brothers or sisters. If as children they felt rejected or spurned for another by

their parents, they may as adults expect the same treatment from their mates.

People with very low self-esteem also tend to be untrusting of their mates. There are large discrepancies between how they see themselves and how they would like to be. A person with this problem usually thinks so little of himself and his "lovability," he believes that if his mate had other choices she would no longer love him. Feeling unworthy of his mate, he expects her to betray him.

They formed "insecure" attachments to their parents.

Most people are given reasonable care in their infancy and have developed "basic trust." As a result, they are able to form attachments to their parents and later to others. However, although basic needs are met by most mothers, mothers are all imperfect and some are more so than others. The quality of mother–child relationships covers a wide range.

Current research has confirmed what psychotherapists have been saying for years, that the kind of attachments formed in early childhood affects adult relationships with mates.

The British psychoanalyst John Bolby described infant–mother attachments as either secure or insecure. He found that intimate attachments to other human beings are important throughout life and that an insecure attachment during infancy permanently affects the future vulnerability of the adult.

Mary Ainsworth, a developmental psychologist, and her colleagues at the University of Virginia classified relationships between toddlers and mothers as secure attachments (about two-thirds of those they saw) and insecure or anxious attachments. The anxious attachment children were either anxious-avoidant—not very much attached to their mothers and easily comforted by a stranger—or anxious-resistant—seeking contact but at the same time resisting their mothers and showing anger when they returned from a brief separation.

Recently, Dr. Phillip Shaver, psychologist, and Cindy Hazan, Research Associate, from the University of Denver tested the theory that the patterns of attachments formed in childhood affect the types of relationships people develop as adults. They found that just over half of their subjects fit into the category of "secure" attachment to their mates, while the rest split evenly between anxious clingers and those who avoid emotional entanglements.

"Securely attached" people felt comfortable getting close to others and had little problem with mutual dependence in relationships. Their relationships lasted longest and seemed happiest.

The group who formed "avoidant" attachments felt uneasy with too much closeness and had difficulty trusting others. They more often reported fears of intimacy and jealousy in their relationships.

Those who formed "anxious/ambivalent" relationships tended to be anxious and clingy, worrying a great deal about being abandoned by lovers. They reported experiencing greater emotional extremes than the other groups. In addition, many in this group expressed the desire to merge with their lovers.

When the subjects recalled their childhoods, each group reported a different picture of their families. Secure lovers saw parents as loving and responsive while anxious lovers gave mixed reports for theirs, tending to view their mothers as emotionally intrusive and their fathers as demanding and distant. They did not see their parents' relationships as happy.

Avoidant people gave conflicting reports. The older ones saw mothers as rejecting and unlikable and fathers as uncaring. The younger ones rated parents just as positively as did secure adults, which Shaver explained as probably due to overidealization of their parents by the younger people. When avoidant people grow older, they probably become more realistic about their parents and consequently more negative.

What exactly is the behavior that makes for a securely attached child? Dr. Ainsworth and her colleagues observed many mothers with their children and noticed that mothers of secure babies were gentler in the way they handled their children, using warmer tones when they gave commands. These mothers were more supportive but appropriately directive. They did more hugging and cuddling than the mothers of anxiously attached babies. A later study showed that mothers of attached-avoidant infants did more kissing than other mothers. The researchers theorized that what children want is close bodily contact, and kissing alone is not what they need. It is also possible that these mothers were smothering and made the children feel uncomfortable because of the anxiety with which they clung to their children. Clinical observation has shown that children of clingy mothers sometimes respond by avoiding too much contact with them.

The important factor in helping children develop a secure attachment is for the parents to respond to their children's needs, rather than their own. Children need to be protected from undue frustration, injury, and unpredictable events. They need to be comforted when in distress and responded to regularly and without long delays. Some parents, because of their own fears, are too responsive to their children. This causes the children to become anxiously attached.

They have been taught by parents not to trust others.
Even children who feel they can trust their parents can learn to distrust others. When children are attached to their parents (securely or insecurely), they tend to adopt their parents' values and attitudes through identification and imitation. Thus, parents who have difficulties with trust convey this to their children either verbally or by example. They transmit the attitude that although they themselves can be trusted, the children should not trust others. This message is communicated whether or not the parents are consciously aware of their own attitudes. Children learn to read their parents' behavior, hidden messages, and attitudes—and learn to distrust.

Sometimes a mother teaches her daughter to be suspicious and untrusting by complaining about her husband's sexual infidelities. She may even verbalize that "you can't trust any men." A child who grows up aware of her father's betrayal of her mother will find it difficult to avoid becoming suspicious of her own husband.

━━

TRUST is not an all-or-none phenomenon. In healthy relationships it generally builds in small increments. To achieve true intimacy, a large measure of trust on both sides is needed.

When someone has problems with trust, for any of the reasons described in this chapter, his suspiciousness and doubt can destroy his intimate relationships. He may avoid relationships entirely (as many Distancers do), protect himself by placing barriers between himself and his mate (as Pseudo-Intimates are likely to do), or drive his partner away because of his endless questioning and nagging (as Intimacy Saboteurs do). By fearing to place his faith in any other person, the person who can't trust deprives himself of any chance of closeness.

7

Fears of Intimacy

While most IAs trust their mates in a fundamental way, they all hold back in at least one area of relating. They all place some barrier between themselves and their mates to prevent full intimacy. Why?

For many of the Intimacy Avoiders the greatest obstacle to closeness is fear. When you scratch the surface of an IA and peel away the excuses and defenses, you usually find some specific fear or fears that prevent total intimacy.

As you saw from their descriptions, IAs' specific fears cross boundaries of personality types. They can be found to a different extent and with different expressions in several types. In addition, they are often disguised. They express themselves in people's behavior and feelings in complex ways. One behavior can represent many fears and one fear can lead to many different reactions depending on the IA's personality. Sometimes these reactions seem contradictory, since you see the IA's defensive behavior rather than direct evidence of the fear itself.

In spite of all these difficulties, certain characteristic patterns emerge. I will elucidate and illustrate some of the most common fears that make lovers become strangers. I'll relate them to the types of IAs that were described in previous chapters.

FEAR OF ABANDONMENT

Some IAs, especially Intimacy Saboteurs, greatly fear abandonment. Sometimes they fear that their loved ones will actually leave them. Other times they fear not physical desertion but psychological withdrawal: will the other be there for them emotionally, to meet their needs and take care of them?

People who are afraid of being abandoned feel unable to survive on their own. They do not trust their own internal resources and believe they need others for their very existence. But they are usually not in touch with this feeling; it is much too threatening for them to realize that underneath their more readily acceptable excuses for avoiding intimacy is this fundamental anxiety.

How do they express this anxiety? Some make sure that they always have safety nets when they enter relationships. The Fickle Lover, for example, limits her dependency on any one lover by having more than one at the same time. If she is abandoned by one, the other is always there for her.

Others, like People Pleasers, Martyrs, and Clingers, ward off abandonment by doing whatever they can to please their mates so they will never be discarded. This usually doesn't quell their fears, however, because they perpetually feel they "have to" please their mates in order to keep them. They always feel at risk and need constant reassurance that their mates will be there for them.

FEAR OF REJECTION

Rejection is difficult for anyone, but some IAs have an unrealistic fear of it. This fear is related to fear of abandonment but is somewhat different. People who fear rejection are afraid that they will not be accepted for what they are. They fear that their needs will be ignored. Even when they are convinced that their partners will not leave them, they may still feel rejected because they are not totally accepted by them.

Many of these people bring rejection on themselves. Since they expect it, they tend to interpret as rejection many things others do. Believing themselves rejected, they may react by withdrawing or becoming angry. Their mates then feel unfairly treated and may retaliate. Most never realize that their behavior is at all connected with the result. They see the rejection as evidence of the correctness of their expectations.

One woman who fears rejection is June. Because of her insecurities, she cannot share her boyfriend with anyone—not his mother, his sister, or his friends. She is jealous of any comment he makes about anyone else, even someone he sees on TV or in the movies. She feels inadequate if a pretty woman is in the same room with her. She worries that the other woman will steal the show and that her boyfriend will prefer this woman to her.

In therapy, she became aware of her overreactions and attempted to control them. Yet her fantasies continued to center around operations to enlarge her breasts or fix her chin, nose, and jaw (all of which are fine). Although she is a very attractive young girl, she feels she has to be the prettiest one around or she will lose love.

FEAR OF ANGER

A characteristic expression of an IA's unconscious fear of rejection or abandonment is overreaction to anger. Some IAs seem to live in trepidation of their mate's anger—as if anger or disapproval will surely lead to abandonment.

Most people who fear others' anger or disapproval do not realize they are threatened. They are able to mask their fear and defend against it by either getting angry at their mates or pacifying them.

Some (People Pleasers and Martyrs, for example) react with compliance, hoping to appease the anger. Many of them go so far as to refrain from saying no as a way to keep their mates from being angry with them.

Others, like the Defiant Disagreers and Mr. Machos, react by becoming outraged that the other person is angry with them. Whether the original anger is justified or not, they are so threatened by it that they cover up with anger returned. They are in effect saying, "How dare you get angry with me and make me feel so frightened?"

Some IAs are aware of being threatened when their partner is angry with them but do not understand why. These people

(Passive Procrastinators, for example) may avoid confrontation because of their fear that their partners will be angry with them. They may avoid making promises or commitments to their mates, to ensure that they won't disappoint them and incur their wrath.

This fear often extends to others who are less important to these IAs. They often tell you that they "hate to be yelled at" or that they "don't want anyone to be angry at them," but they usually can't verbalize what it is they actually fear. Nonetheless, in all of these situations, the IAs' reactions to their fears act as a wedge between them and their mates.

Why should these IAs be so much afraid of their mates' anger? Perhaps the anger reminds them of their parents, who were in a position to physically hurt them, deprive them, or abandon them. Just as they feared their parents' anger when they were children (because of what might result from this anger), as adults they fear their partners' displeasure. It is likely that these people still feel as vulnerable as they did when they were children.

What makes some people so overly sensitive to rejection or abandonment? Most children are not actually abandoned or rejected outright. Their fears of rejection or abandonment come from subtle things their parents have done to them.

The type of early relationships people have with their parents determines how secure they feel in their attachments and how much they fear rejection or abandonment. If their attachments to their parents were warm, loving, and full of acceptance, their later experiences will be similar. On the other hand, those who were victims of neglect or hostility often grow up to treat loved ones with neglect or hostility and to expect to be treated the same way.

Research reported by Dr. Phillip Shaver of the University of Denver (referred to in the chapter on Trust) showed that a child who grows up feeling rejected by a parent of the opposite sex is prone to extremes of jealousy, anxiety, and depression in adult love life. This can be diminished if the person understands the origins of his or her feelings.

Similarly, Dr. Carl Hindy, a psychologist at the University of North Florida in Jacksonville, found that women whose fathers were detached, hostile, or inconsistent were found to be more insecure as adults in love relationships.

Fear of rejection can come from having very controlling parents. Many parents use subtle withdrawal of love and attention as a method of control. When the child doesn't do what they expect and want, they withdraw and act as if they don't love or like the child or want to be with him. This is very effective in getting children to become docile and obedient. However, a serious side effect of this treatment is that it makes the children forever sensitive to rejection and insecure about their basic ability to be lovable. These children always feel that their parents' love is conditional on their living up to the parents' expectations—no matter how difficult or unrealistic. Often parents who treat their children this way expect the children to fulfill the parents' own needs and feel very threatened when the children try to assert their individuality and autonomy.

Others who fear rejection feel inadequate and are waiting to be "found out." Some feel bad about themselves because their parents were too critical. They internalized their parents' criticism and became very critical of themselves (and, incidentally, of others as well).

Some people feel inadequate and fear rejection not because their parents were critical or controlling, but because they were unavailable, due to overwork, depression, divorce, or other reasons. Children can't understand why they aren't played with or given more attention. They tend to conclude that it is because they are unlovable or bad. They feel that if they were good enough their parents would give them more time and love. Even after they grow up, they still carry this feeling with them—and expect to be rejected.

FEAR OF CRITICISM

Getting close to others means disclosing a great deal about yourself. It also means allowing them—and what they think—to become important to you. While this is a risk for everybody, for those who fear criticism the risk is even greater. This fear is prevalent in the Sensitive Sulker, the Social Butterfly, and the Do-

Gooder. These people are always concerned about others' seeing their faults and weaknesses. They tend to anticipate criticism as well as fear it. No wonder they are reluctant to get close and leave themselves open to scrutiny.

How does someone's fear of criticism interfere with relating? For one thing, it makes it very difficult for others to express the most minor complaint about them or to ask something different of them, whether it be in bed, in the kitchen, or in the back yard. Anything partners request may be seen as criticism, and thus they frequently feel they can have no input with regard to their IA spouses' behavior.

In an attempt to ward off criticism, these IAs cause great difficulties in their relationships. Some of them react to criticism by becoming angry and shouting. They feel they have to loudly protect themselves from what they view as an attack. Others play weak and helpless, hoping to avoid the blow by making their mates feel guilty and sorry for them.

Neither of these methods protects the person from the on-slaught of criticism; the critic's anger only increases. Under circumstances such as these, any attempt to communicate becomes destructive and only serves to drive a wedge between the people rather than help understanding.

Why are some people so afraid of criticism? Usually they have very low self-esteem, which in some cases is covered with a thin veneer of self-confidence. In order for them to feel good about themselves, they cannot make a mistake. These people are so perfectionistic in whatever they undertake, they are never quite able to please themselves. They cannot forgive themselves for not being perfect. When someone else points out that something they did is flawed, even in a minor way, they react as if they are being told they are utterly worthless. Since they are prone to seeing things in the extreme—either black or white—any criticism seems catastrophic to them. Because they are ready to believe the worst of themselves, they think that others believe it also, but it is their own bad feelings about themselves that they attempt to counteract rather than the other person's opinion.

How fear of criticism can destroy intimacy is easily seen in the case of John. When his wife, Doris, had any complaints about his behavior, he would get extremely angry. He felt she was saying that he was "no good." For example, after a party, Doris complained that John didn't help enough with the cleaning up. He reacted as if she had said he didn't do anything the entire evening to help and never did anything to help her. John was reacting to his fears rather than the reality of the situation. Instead of attempting to understand the actual complaint and perhaps rectify it, he made matters worse by getting angry at his wife for criticizing him.

Because of John's basic feelings of inadequacy, he is very quick to believe negative comments about himself. When he was young, his mother constantly found fault with him as well as with his sister and his father. She criticized and even ridiculed him whenever he tried anything new. Yet she never criticized him for doing nothing—for just being there, dependent on her. If he did as little as possible, but was loyal and dependent, he would get love. Of course, although at home that might have worked, when he went out in the world this behavior was not rewarded. He did not develop a feeling of competence and was afraid of trying new things because he felt that he would surely fail and thus be open to ridicule.

Since his mother never expected much from him, he is surprised and resentful when his wife expects his help. If Doris loved him, he reasons, she would not expect him to do what he finds uncomfortable. When he does attempt to please her, it takes more effort for him to overcome his fears and hesitancy than she could ever appreciate. Any negative comments are enough to discourage him. On one hand, he feels she is never satisfied with him or his efforts; on the other hand, he feels totally inadequate and resents her for confronting him with that feeling. Doris becomes frustrated because she cannot complain to him about anything without causing a battle. Neither is satisfied and both end up feeling resentful and angry.

In therapy, John became aware of the reasons for his inability to deal with criticism and how it was interfering with intimate relating. When he was able to acknowledge that his interpretation of Doris's complaints as faultfinding was wrong, he was better able to handle the disagreements and complaints. He learned to distinguish between her general frustration and her discontent with his behavior. He learned to evaluate what she was saying in terms of what she really wanted from him. He began to see that a critique of his behavior was not a total "put down" of him. As a result of these insights, and his work on building his self-esteem, their marriage improved enormously.

FEAR OF BEING CONTROLLED

Many IAs express the fear of being controlled by their loved ones. They worry that they will be inhibited from doing what they like with their time, their money, and their lives. While sometimes this concern is realistic, as when they are involved with Tyrants or similarly demanding people, often these fears are rooted in their own psyches. Why do some people have such an inordinate fear of losing their autonomy?

Many of those who fear being controlled don't trust their ability to stand up for their own rights and needs. Because of their overpowering need for their mates' approval, love, and good-will, they very much need to please them, and so they feel forced or obligated to do what their mates say.

These people are usually too dependent on their mates and feel too needy to risk their displeasure. Their partners can easily manipulate these IAs with threats of leaving, withholding of love, or angry outbursts. Some may try to make their partners feel sorry for them or threaten to become depressed or sick.

People who fear being controlled often need to be in control themselves. Only when they regulate situations and relationships can they be comfortable and anxiety-free. They pride themselves on being restrained at all times and on having all their affairs in order. In this way, they ensure that no mistakes are made and that all their needs are met. This is most obvious in the Intellectualizer, who always needs to maintain his control and keep his feelings in check.

When dealing with others on an intimate level, everyone has to give up some control. Even when partners are very reasonable, relationships require compromise and the sharing of decision making. This is difficult for those who need to maintain a close check on everything around them. They view whatever their partners ask for as inordinate demands.

The person who fears being controlled is often very careful

about spending money. He is usually a hard worker, sometimes to a fault (as is the Workaholic), and is rigid and perfectionistic with himself and others (like the Perfectionist, the Constant Critic, and the Intellectualizer). Since he needs to be right all the time, he is unlikely to admit mistakes and is usually intolerant of others' mistakes, feeling a sense of moral indignation when things aren't done "just right."

Although they rarely express this or admit it, except after years of therapy, many who fear being controlled really want to control their mates. This is most apparent in Mr. Machos, Tyrants, and Constant Critics. Despite the fact that it may go against their own moral judgment, these IAs frequently feel that they "have to" control their mates' behavior in order to appease their fears and meet their needs. It is very frightening for them to leave things to others. Their only alternative is to fully take control of the situation and of their mates. These IAs are frequently unaware that their behavior is so controlling. They accept the behavior because they don't realize the motives for it.

Those who fear being controlled were usually raised by controlling mothers. Harsh toilet training is often blamed for this condition, but it is usually more complicated than that. The mother who put her young child through rigid potty training also demanded other controls from the child. It is likely that she insisted that most things were done to her specifications, no matter how difficult for the child. He wasn't allowed to dirty the furniture, mess up the house, or refuse to obey her. She undoubtedly got into a power struggle with all but the most compliant child. The only way such a child could express his autonomy and aggression was through passive means such as withholding.

People raised in that kind of an atmosphere learn that self-control and restraint are necessary to gain love and approval. Out of this developed their strong need to be in control at all times and in all situations. In addition, they learned to suppress their anger so that it would not sabotage their relationships with their mothers and, later, with their lovers.

When these children mature, they are always on guard against those who threaten to control them. They are continually vigilant of others whom they love, fearing that their beloveds, like their mothers, will take away their autonomy.

FEAR OF MERGING

In some people the fear of control reaches such proportions that they fear being taken over by others to whom they are close. They worry about losing their integrity. Yet, at the same time they want and need closeness and may even want to merge with, or become part of, their lover. These people often have difficulty knowing who they are and what they stand for. When they get very close to someone, they fear becoming an appendage to that person. Any time a partner asks anything of them they feel that they must comply. But they are apprehensive that if they do what their lover demands (or even requests), they will no longer be able to be themselves.

Andy had great conflicts in his marriage as a result of his fear of merging. When he and Jane were first married, they were together constantly. It seemed that they could hardly do anything without each other. Then problems began. Andy started having anxiety attacks when Jane wasn't home and when they went on trips. He began therapy and came to realize that his anxiety represented a fear of separation from his wife and from home. Even after he was in therapy for a while, Andy would feel compelled to call Jane several times a day to check in. If he didn't call, Jane would call him.

Although afraid of separation, Andy was not comfortable with so much closeness. He maintained his distance by not feeling sexual toward Jane and by having fantasies of other women when they did have sex. He said that after having intercourse with Jane, he would be afraid of going to sleep because of fantasies of being "swallowed up." While Andy desired closeness, he also feared the loss of his own integrity, which he believed would result from the closeness. So he alternately got extremely close or backed away.

Andy became aware of his problem and how it was affecting his relationship and his peace of mind. In therapy, he was able to understand and finally overcome these feelings. Andy worked on his own sense of himself as a separate person. When he felt good enough about himself to risk standing alone, he was more able to be close to his wife without feeling threatened.

In some sense we all wish to merge with—be one with—our loves. We wish to return to the idyllic period of prenatal times and infancy when we were inseparable from our mothers and all our needs were instantly and unquestioningly met. Yet, for an adult that state can also be threatening. The feeling of losing yourself—disappearing or no longer being your own person—is very frightening.

People who have difficulty balancing intimacy with individuality, or who fear they can't maintain their integrity in a relationship, have never completely differentiated or separated from their mothers, who usually needed to keep them close and under their control. Mothers like theirs are always telling their offspring what they should think, like, want, and feel. "Wear this outfit, you don't know what's nice to wear" or "Eat this, it tastes good; you don't know what's good" (or "what you like"). Some children of such mothers set up very strong boundaries and defenses (and become wary of being controlled in later relationships). They are the children who become stubborn and either overtly or passively rebellious—for example, by refusing to eat or to go to the bathroom on schedule. Children who are more compliant or passive accept their mothers' control and never fully become their own persons. As adults they are frequently afraid of merging and losing themselves in a relationship.

FEAR OF DEPLETION

In intimate relationships, the amount and type of giving and receiving are very subjective and not well defined. This causes problems for many people who are afraid of giving too much and not getting enough in return.

Most IAs who have difficulties with giving feel extremely needy. They have a profound conviction that they do not have enough resources even for themselves, much less for someone else—everything they need must be given to them. Thus, they dare not give to another for fear of absolute depletion. Yet, in spite of their great needs, they sometimes have difficulty accepting from others. They fear that others will want more of them than they can give. They worry that the "price" they will have to pay for what they get may be higher than they can afford.

When IAs who fear depletion give to others or do what others want in order to get affection, they become resentful and often appear depressed. They deplore being enslaved and having to comply but sometimes do so because they fear losing their mates. Not knowing that it is their own anxiety that brings on this situation, they blame the other person.

These IAs are generally convinced that others will not give back to them. Because they feel so needy, they tend to have unreasonable expectations of others and are intolerant of others' inadequacies or flaws. They interpret other people's actions in such a way as to reinforce their belief that they get nothing from them. Sometimes they look for very specific evidence of "giving" and don't recognize what is given to them in a less obvious form. Or, they expect more than others can reasonably give. In either case, they maintain that they are not given to, even when it is not entirely true.

When others do give to them, people who fear depletion often become suspicious. They fear that the givers want something from them or are somehow gaining advantages by being nice to them. This belief makes it difficult to accept what is being offered.

While it is normal to want to be loved for what you are and not for what you can do for others, those who fear depletion exaggerate this desire to mean that they should be loved without any return or advantage to their mates.

In order to ensure that their mates don't merely want them for what they can do for them, they limit the amount that they give. If a mate gains anything from the relationship, the IA suspects that the gain is the mate's only motivation for remaining involved.

These IAs also want unconditional love. They expect their partners to love them no matter how little they give, no matter how provocatively they act toward them, and no matter what sacrifices the partners are required to make. They set up an impossible situation and thus ensure that no one can prove their love for them.

They also avoid anything that may be construed as "giving in" and letting their partners have their way. Doing so makes them feel as if they are being controlled. Like those who fear being controlled, these IAs need to always be in control of their relationships in order to make sure that they get what they need.

Allowing their mates' needs to dominate, even for a moment, represents a threat to them. Usually they are not aware that they are always insisting on their own way. They see each instance of their partners' wanting their way as an effort to take control. On each occasion, they feel that they, rather than their partners, should prevail.

Most IAs who fear depletion confuse need with love, believing that because they greatly need their partners, this means that they love them. However, their predominant feeling is merely gratitude for being loved or cared for. For most of us love isn't purely altruistic and sacrificing; we want certain things from our beloved, such as gratification, loyalty, help. However, the person who fears depletion needs affection as a defense against anxiety, and as a result tends to cling to and become very demanding of his mate. He is usually not concerned about his partner's personality, limitations, needs, wishes, or development. (A drowning person can hardly be concerned about whether his savior is capable of or willing to carry him.) These IAs are hardly ever aware of their real incapacity for love or giving. They need others and so have to hide their hostility even from themselves. Their feelings may be covered up by desperate attempts to be considerate, but true feelings come out in disguised ways.

Carol is a young woman who appears to have all the assets necessary for a good relationship. A professional woman in her mid-thirties, she lives alone, owns her own home, and has a good job. She has many friends and is attractive and vivacious. She is also very popular with men and has many dates. Her problems begin when her relationships become serious. In the beginning of a relationship, when she feels insecure with her lover, she is easygoing and compliant. However, this causes her to feel resentful. Once she feels more secure with her lover, she can express her true feelings. As soon as she senses that he is "hooked on her," she can afford to get openly angry with him. She becomes very demanding and withholding. If he doesn't respond and seems to back off, she holds back her anger. She then becomes depressed, presenting herself as weak, helpless, and sick. Sometimes her lovers respond to that for a while, but as soon as she feels secure, she becomes demanding and inconsiderate again.

Her relationships are often stormy and rarely go beyond this initial stage. Even when men put up with her demands for a while, they finally get upset with her selfishness and leave. Why does she so resent being giving and compromising with a man?

Carol is a frightened, needy woman. She was brought up to be suspicious of others' taking advantage of her. She is afraid of giving because she is afraid of being depleted. She is deeply convinced that she doesn't have enough resources even for herself, much less for someone else.

Carol does not see herself as nongiving; people rarely do. She is aware that she resents doing things that her boyfriends want and has great difficulty understanding their needs or problems. But she says that it is because they want too much from her and do not give enough themselves.

Carol has been working on her own inner feelings of insecurity and has been learning how to feed herself emotionally. As she has improved herself in therapy, and begun to feel less needy, her relationships have gradually improved.

Why do people fear depletion?   Usually those who fear depletion did not experience enough giving when they were very young. Their parents were either unavailable or psychologically unable to nurture them adequately, and they grew up feeling hurt and vulnerable, needing all that they could get from others. In their adult relationships they often try to make up for their earlier deprivation. They expect their mates to give them what they couldn't get as infants. And, like infants, they can't give back.

When their mates are very giving, they may be superficially and temporarily reassured, but these IAs are still suspicious because they anticipate being deprived and frustrated. As a result of their early experiences, they feel undeserving of love and attention, so they are distrustful of it even when authentic. Others' affection arouses additional fears of dependency—because their need is so great they have to ward it off and deny it.

❦❦❦❦——————————————————————————

FEARS OF CLOSENESS cause people to erect the biggest and thickest veils between themselves and their partners. This chapter has described the most common of these fears—abandoment,

rejection, criticism, being controlled, merging, and depletion—
and explained how people develop these fears in childhood.

Those who experience these fears try to protect themselves
from awareness of their fears as well as from being hurt by others.
But all of their defensive reactions merely serve to distance them
from their mates and sometimes bring on the very thing they
most dread—abandonment.

8

Overdependency

It is easy to see why a mate who is afraid of closeness can feel like a stranger in your bed. The fear stands between the two of you, creating an impenetrable barrier. But dependency doesn't appear to prohibit closeness—it even seems to enhance it. After all, if you didn't need each other you wouldn't be together.

Dependency itself doesn't present a barrier to intimacy. Relationships require some degree of mutual dependence. We all need some encouragement and help from our mates. But those who are overly dependent take this a step further: they need others to feel complete. Being part of another, stronger person helps them feel protected and secure. Overdependent people often don't trust their own judgment or abilities. Believing they could not survive on their own, they fear being without their mates' total support. As a result, overdependent people don't avoid closeness, they desperately seek it. But because of the desperation in their quest, and because they are not strong enough to hold their end, they often sabotage their relationships.

WHAT ARE SOME OF THE PROBLEMS CAUSED BY OVERDEPENDENCY?

Incompetent Behavior

Although some dependent people are quite capable of taking care of themselves, at least functionally, many have large areas of incapacity. Some women feel they should be totally supported financially (even when they don't have young children and can earn their own living). Others feel incapable of driving a car or of going anywhere alone. Still others think they are unable to call a repairman by themselves. Men sometimes act as if they can't cook for themselves (or learn to) or do their own laundry. They can't find anything in their own home and need their wives to make a sandwich for them.

These overdependents frequently seek mates who will do things for them. But the relationship is never completely satisfying; it only increases their feelings of inadequacy. Waiting for others to do for them, constantly having to ask, beg, or demand that others do for them, does not build self-esteem or feelings of security. And no matter how good they are at manipulating others, they never fully have what they want. What they fail to realize is what the average two-year-old knows instinctively: it is better to be autonomous.

Expecting others to take care of them places strains on the overdependents' relationships. Even if their mates are very giving and nurturing, caretaking is never without conditions, explicit or implicit. Certain behaviors are expected of them in return, which overdependents resent since they feel they were never—not even as children—given to without "strings." Their often unexpressed fantasies are that they are still children and should be treated as such. Yet when they have mates who do treat them like children (with all the control of parents) they strongly resent it.

Demanding, Overcritical Behavior

Many overdependent IAs feel deprived and depleted. They expect and often demand that their mates make this up to them. Clingers and Sensitive Sulkers make whiney or sometimes unspoken demands, whereas Tyrants are aggressive in ordering their mates around. Because they count on them to fulfill their needs, over-dependents have unusually strict requirements of their partners. Spouses are required to be strong, without flaws or needs of their own. Nevertheless, things are not always done exactly the way dependent mates want them, so spouses are usually criticized in spite of their good points. This is expressed passively by Clingers and overtly by Tyrants.

Constant Need for Emotional Support

Some overdependents can take care of themselves physically (or financially) but can't think for themselves or feel secure by them-selves. Their neediness consists of endless pleas for approval, reassurance, and help with decision making.

These IAs require constant proof of their desirability. They continually ask their mates questions such as, "Do you love me?" or "Do you think I'm pretty (or handsome, or sexy)?"

When they have to make a decision about anything at all, they feel unable to make it alone. Yet, although wanting their partners' support and encouragement, they often reject their ad-vice and ask others'. They might ask their parents and friends, the neighbors, and the children, and still feel unable to decide.

Trying to meet the insatiable needs of overdependents is extremely frustrating for their partners. No amount of reassur-ance or approval is enough for someone who doesn't really believe it. This type of overdependence is often seen in Clingers, People Pleasers, Martyrs, and other types of Intimacy Saboteurs.

Overcompliance

Overdependence often leads to inordinate fears of abandonment and rejection. To ward off these fears, some overdependents be-come very compliant. People Pleasers are the most consistently compliant, but Martyrs, Clingers, Passive Procrastinators, and Sensitive Sulkers can also be submissive.

Eventually, submissive people become resentful. They begin to withdraw from their loved ones, or they get "sick" or depressed. Sometimes they "get even" with passive aggressive behavior (for example, by "forgetting" to do something important for their mates or by falling asleep early every night).

HOW PEOPLE HIDE OVERDEPENDENCY

Some of the Intimacy Avoiders, such as Clingers, People Pleasers, and Sensitive Sulkers, are obviously overdependent. They may view their dependent longings as natural and acceptable. Others, especially men and "liberated" women, feel ashamed of their dependency. Although these people really want to be taken care of, they find their dependent feelings hard to admit even to themselves. They disguise their dependency behind stereotypes and excuses, such as "Men are supposed to pay for women," or "It is a woman's job to cook and clean," or "He won't let me pay the bills, get a job, pay for dinner, et cetera—it would hurt his masculinity," or "I can't go off on my own because of the children."

Some IAs hide their dependency from themselves by marrying someone who needs to take care of them. As long as both people agree, this can work out very well. Usually the stronger partner assumes the role of parent to the other. The parent partner gains control of the relationship because he is the one who gives the most and needs the least (on the surface, at least). The dependent partner is willing to give up control in order to be taken care of.

Other overdependents are more subtle. They marry someone who seems on the surface to be more dependent than themselves. This ensures that they are never abandoned. While to the world it may appear that these IAs are the caretakers, in reality they are just as needful of their mates as their mates are of them. This subterfuge is employed by Mr. Machos, Rescuers, and sometimes Workaholics.

Another common ploy of overdependents is to spread themselves out among many lovers, because they fear having to depend too much on any one person. Their neediness is then somewhat disguised, but these IAs cannot fool others or themselves for long, because of their extreme and desperate need for others to take care of them, in the most basic sense. This description can be true for Fickle Lovers, Affair Seekers, and Perfectionists.

HOW DO PEOPLE BECOME OVERDEPENDENT?

Because of the cultural value placed on being independent, many people, especially men, are reluctant to admit any wish to be dependent on others. Yet, in spite of our carefully constructed facades of independence, deep down in all of us is a great need and desire to be taken care of. We frequently judge our mates' love for us by how much they provide for us emotionally, physically, and materially. While the type of help expected from mates may be different for men and women—women may expect financial support while men expect more physical caretaking such as cooking and cleaning—they both in their own way want someone to care for them.

Being taken care of and being loved are very much associated in our minds. When we were infants and young children, they were one and the same, and our lives literally depended on them both.

In spite of the obvious comfort of complete caretaking, as children grow, they attempt to do more and more for themselves. From the first time children try to walk by themselves, dress themselves, and feed themselves, they are reaching for independence. They strive for independence for many reasons. When they can do more for themselves, they ensure that their needs are met—the means are totally within their control. In addition, they gain a sense of mastery and increased self-esteem. These feelings of independence and need for autonomy can grow and thrive with time or they can wither. In order to grow, they must be encouraged by parents.

Studies of securely and insecurely attached children show that the more securely attached are more independent and seem freer than children who are anxiously attached. Securely attached children suffer less from separation anxiety. Having a secure base enables them to venture away from their mothers. It also seems to influence their later competence in dealing with their environment.

Other studies show that children who have had attention from their fathers as well as their mothers seem more amenable to being left with others. The more experience they have with different people, the better the children's ability to cope with separation and independence.

Dr. D.W. Winnicott, a British psychoanalyst, coined the often quoted term, the "good enough mother," to describe the type of mother who best encourages her child's growth. She begins by almost completely adapting to her infant's needs, but as the infant grows she adapts less and less. She gives less as the infant learns to tolerate more. The child thus slowly gives up his idea of his mother doing everything for him. Dr. Winnicott says that a mother has to give enough, but not too much, for the child to become independent.

Unfortunately, not all mothers fit Winnicott's description of "good enough." For many reasons they thwart their children's growth toward independence. As a consequence, many adults still feel as they did when they were children—that their lives depend upon being cared for and loved. Some of these people feel so inadequate and helpless that they believe they can't take care of themselves. And others, who believe they can fulfill their own needs, are still reluctant to do so. They are afraid to give up their dependency on others. Their association of being loved and being taken care of is so strong that they fear that taking care of themselves means that others will no longer love them.

How is a healthy need for autonomy thwarted, causing some people to cling desperately to the dependent ties that restrict their freedom?

Overprotective Parents

Children don't have to be insecure in their early relationships to grow up overdependent or fearful. They may have developed very secure attachments to parents who needed them to remain dependent. When independent behavior is discouraged or disparaged by parents, children do not try. When independent behavior threatens loss of love, children give it up very quickly.

This can come about when overprotective parents do too much for their children, making them feel they cannot do for themselves. Parents such as these need to take care of their children even after the children no longer require it. These parents are so needy emotionally that they try to hold their children close to them by keeping them dependent. As a result, they don't reward their children's efforts to grow. Their children often feel they have to allow the parents to do for them so that the parents can love them.

Other overprotective parents do too much because they are so dependent on their children's approval that they cannot say no to their demands. Consequently, they "spoil" their children and make them dependent. Then they feel obligated to take care of these incompetent, weak creatures. Some of these parents spoil their children out of guilt for not giving them their attention at times when it was important. They try to make up for their neglect of their children by doing too much or expecting too little. Others spoil their children because they are too busy to take the time and energy to enforce limits.

A third type of overprotective parent feels very helpless and inadequate. Parents in this group overidentify with their children's feelings of helplessness, and instead of encouraging their children to develop, they "protect" them from being hurt or disappointed. These parents make their children dependent by not expecting enough from them, sending the message that if things are too difficult, they should give up. When their children attempt to do things by themselves, the parents often become unduly critical, undermining the children's already fragile confidence and determination. They often paint a frightening picture of the world to their children, who then become timid about facing the "cruel world" alone and choose to stay tied to their parents. Since the parents themselves feel inadequate, they don't offer much security for their children, further increasing their children's anxiety.

Sometimes parents become overprotective because their child appears so fragile. Perhaps the child has been ill much of the time or has been overly fearful of people or new experiences. More and more research shows us that children come into the world with their own distinct temperaments. Dr. Alexander Thomas and Dr. Stella Chess of NYU Medical Center were prominent in studying temperamental differences in infants. Since their early work there have been many other studies showing inborn or very early developing differences among infants, most of which remain as children grow older. Children vary in aggressiveness, sociability, fearfulness, passivity, reactiveness, and other traits. Some children are naturally more compliant and eager to please, while others are more defiant.

Parents are affected by differences in their children's temperaments and frequently treat them differently. The parents' reactions can either strengthen or weaken their children's natural characteristics. For example, if a child is fearful and clingy and his mother is gently encouraging, he is more likely to risk independent behavior. If his mother responds by overprotection or fearfulness, he will stay dependent on her too long and perhaps grow up to be overdependent on others. On the other hand, a more active, outgoing child can overcome an overprotective mother's effects. He might even feel more comfortable risking her disapproval to become more autonomous. The final result—the child's personality—is formed by an interaction between the child's inborn tendencies and his early experiences with parents (and sometimes others).

Underprotective Parents

Some overdependent people were insecurely attached to their parents when they were young. They developed a clingy, anxious relationship with their parents and continue it in later life with their mates. They are likely to have had parents who, for one reason or other, didn't give them enough nurturing or a strong enough sense of security.

Parents who are underprotective, who ignore or neglect their children, leave them feeling hungry for others to take care of them. These parents usually have their own serious problems. They may be depressed or physically or emotionally ill, or they may be too involved with themselves or their mates. They generally have serious problems with intimacy. A child who is raised by parents such as these may learn to take care of himself physically. However, he remains very needy and dependent emotionally. Although chronologically an adult, he is a child in his constant search for others who will be "better parents."

Some of these insecurely attached children will respond to their upbringing by becoming more avoidant in relating to others. They will be the ones who withdraw into themselves or things (toys or books as a child; work as an adult) rather than become

clingy and dependent. These children can become more emotionally self-sufficient or learn how to reduce their own needs to
avoid the pain of rejection.

WHILE DEPENDENCY may appear to foster intimacy, too much
of it can strangle a relationship. In this chapter, we have seen the
various ways in which people develop into overdependents and
how their overdependency can sabotage the very relationships
they feel they desperately need for survival. By their clingy, demanding, or nagging behavior, these Intimacy Saboteurs make
true intimacy impossible.

9

Self-Esteem
and Identity

SELF-ESTEEM

Having a sense of personal worth—high self-esteem—is necessary for any close interaction. Without it people are vulnerable to manipulation by others and risk overdependence on them for approval and acceptance.

Those who lack self-esteem frequently also lack a sense of control over their destiny; they do not feel that they can manage their lives or their relationships. Although low self-esteem is found in all types of IAs, it is most prevalent in Intimacy Saboteurs.

HOW LOW SELF-ESTEEM AFFECTS RELATIONSHIPS

Overdependence on Others for Self-Worth

Those with little self-esteem frequently look to their mates for their sense of worth instead of looking within themselves. As a result, they may choose mates based on the mates' ability to enhance their status rather than because of emotional compatibility or closeness. Some of them, customarily women because of cultural factors, marry successful men, hoping that by association they will become successful. They may, for example, choose Workaholics, Mr. Machos, or Status Seekers, because of these IAs' external trappings. But while they may gain prestige and financial advantages, they rarely feel more valuable or important. In fact, they often feel worse, since their mates' success underlines their own sense of inadequacy. In addition, the men these women choose are usually too busy meeting their own needs for status and power to help their partners or meet their requirements for closeness. This often causes the women to become angry with their husbands for not fulfilling their expectations.

People with little self-esteem sometimes expect their mates to help them achieve—socially, emotionally, or professionally. In other words, they expect their successful mates to teach them to be successful. Placing themselves in a position inferior to their mates'—similar to a student and mentor—makes them very vulnerable to their mates' approval or disapproval and leads to an unequal partnership not conducive to true intimacy.

Extreme Vulnerability to Criticism

Those who don't feel good about themselves tend to exaggerate negative comments made about them. Because they feel bad about themselves, these people expect others to judge them harshly and they tend to interpret their partners' advice or help as criticism or belittlement. The criticism strikes a familiar chord in their own unconscious. When criticized, they feel found out, exposed, to themselves as well as to others. They have great difficulty accepting their own limitations and faults while maintaining good feelings about themselves. This conflict can lead to much unjustified anger and resentment toward their mates—feelings that obviously stand in the way of true intimacy. Overreaction to possible criticism is most prevalent in Sensitive Sulkers.

Easily Manipulated by Others

People with a poor self-image run the risk of allowing themselves to be used. They have an excessive need to buy friendship by doing too much for others or by flattering them, hoping to win them over. In addition, it is difficult for them to assert their own needs. Their partners are always assumed to be right and to know better than they do. As a result, they are reluctant to take a stand and ask for what they want.

People with such problems tend to present themselves as unworthy and less than what they really are. They doubt others' praise and feel too grateful for their mates' love. By underestimating their own strengths, they may take a secondary position, allowing their mates to lead most of the time. This acquiescence tends to get them involved with Tyrants or Mr. Machos who will tell them what to do, but mates such as these only intensify the feelings of inadequacy in people with low self-esteem, causing them to become even more passive and dependent on their mates.

Doubting their own judgment, and always needing confirmation from others, they hesitate about making decisions. They might become clingy, like the Clinger, or always try to second-guess their partners, like the People Pleaser. Either reaction can cause their partners to become chronically upset with them for their apparent inadequacy.

People with such problems might also forgo taking credit for their own achievements, which leads to resentment and increases their feelings of unworthiness. People Pleasers, Martyrs, and Clingers exemplify this behavior. Many are prone to depression and have difficulty recovering from failures, however small, because they see them as evidence of unworthiness. Because they can't accept even their minor limitations, these people usually expect more from themselves than do those with high self-esteem.

Overpossessive Behavior

People with poor self-images are frequently vulnerable to fears of rejection. Finding it hard to believe their mates care for them, like the Constant Clinger they require constant reassurance of their mates' love. They can become overpossessive of their mates' time and jealous or envious of others. Since they feel they can't compete with others, they are easily threatened if their mates notice or comment about another's looks, intelligence, or success.

Some become preoccupied with the idea of losing their mates and can become Jealous Doubters.

Devaluation of Their Mates

Some people who have low self-esteem devalue others who care for them. They can be similar to Romanticists, who can love only those who are unavailable or not interested in them. Or they may make the unconscious assumption that if their mates are willing to accept them (as inadequate as they believe themselves to be) their mates must also be deficient.

People of this type who marry never quite accept their choices. They are continually angry with their spouses because they feel "stuck." Fearing they can't do any better, they stay in unhappy relationships.

Defensiveness Against Feelings of Inferiority

The other side of the coin of a poor self-image is the defensive reaction against it. People who have to defend against feelings of inadequacy sometimes become Workaholics or Status Seekers—driven to show off materially (buying expensive and unnecessary things) or intellectually to combat their fears about themselves. They are afraid to look bad in others' eyes, so they exaggerate their own importance. Their ambitiousness and sense of "pride" may be extreme, to make up for unconscious fears about their true worth, and they may try to impress others in trivial ways—by name-dropping or excessive tipping, for example. Some overdefend against any authority. "No one can tell me what to do. Who do they think they are?"

Others, such as Narcissists, may appear to have exalted opinions of themselves and everyone connected with them. They tend to idealize and exalt their mates, but only as long as their mates never disagree with them. However, sometimes those who are defending against feelings of low self-esteem put down their partners because they feel (wrongly) that this makes them look better in others' eyes. Mr. Macho is an example of this type. So is the Constant Critic. In addition, some who drive themselves and those around them toward perfection do so to counteract feelings of inadequacy. Perfectionists are like this: in defending against feelings of low self-esteem, they can't ever find partners good enough to make up for their own feelings of inadequacy.

HOW DO PEOPLE DEVELOP A SELF-IMAGE?

People develop their feelings about themselves in childhood, through their interpretation of their parents' opinions of them. If parents attribute lack of ability to their children, the children don't try. On the other hand, confidence in their children's ability can be conveyed by encouraging remarks such as, "You can do it. All you have to do is apply yourself."

Some parents think well of their children, but because they don't communicate these feelings or the children don't perceive them, the children never develop self-esteem. Why would parents not let their children know how they feel?

Some parents consciously discourage children from feeling too good about themselves. They have the mistaken notion that this leads to less effort from their children and a lack of humility—a "big head"—and lessens the parents' authority. Whenever their children express pride in themselves or their achievements, the parents discourage them through embarrassment or guilt.

Other parents want their children to develop self-esteem but don't want to reward them too easily. These parents are generally very exacting and easily find fault with their inexperienced children. Instead of encouraging their children's efforts to be independent, they become even more disapproving, believing that if they reward imperfect behavior, they will discourage their children from trying harder to succeed.

When children don't meet parental standards, however high or unrealistic, they develop poor self-images. If they have inflexible parents or are constantly told they're "bad" when they have disobeyed their mothers by, for example, not eating their cereal or not doing well in school, they grow up feeling inadequate. The feeling persists even if they believe their parents love them.

Children see their parents as perfect and themselves as weak and flawed. Consequently, when their parents don't approve of them, they assume it is due to their own inadequacies rather than their parents' faultfinding or overperfectionism. They learn to expect perfection from themselves, becoming as hard on themselves and as unforgiving as their parents were. When they become adults, they transfer those expectations onto those around them and find it difficult to accept flaws and limitations in their mates or their own children.

On the other hand, some parents don't set standards at all. Believing they are being very accepting and permissive, they don't expect enough from their children (considering their children's abilities, of course). Consequently, although these children may feel good about themselves when they are very young, later in life when they enter school or the workplace they don't strive hard enough and consequently don't meet societal standards. They become "underachievers" who attribute their lack of success to society, "bad luck," lack of opportunity, or themselves.

Children who have an overidealized conception of their parents (or one of their parents) also can develop poor self-images. They never recognize their parents' faults. They continue, well past the point of adolescence and adulthood, to view their parents in an overidealized way. Perhaps their mothers were presented as "saints" and their fathers were "no good." Or their mothers were unaccommodating and their fathers were wonderful. Such a dichotomy is sometimes encouraged by one parent, who is closer to the child and "protects" him from the other parent. Other times, the overidealized parent is the less available one, as happens when a father is successful at work and not home very much, or is unavailable because of divorce or death. Because the child can never live up to this wonderful parent's image, he always feels inadequate.

Children can also develop low self-esteem by identifying with parents whom they see as weak and incompetent or who themselves have low self-esteem. These parents often don't expect much from their children because they don't expect much from themselves (either realistically or unrealistically). As a result, the children don't develop confidence in their abilities. Parents such as these may be too lenient in setting limits, trying to make up for their inability to give more or be more for their children. Because they don't earn respect from their children, the children grow up to be adults who find it hard to respect themselves.

Parents help their children develop their sense of control in the world. Through interaction with their parents, children develop a sense of who makes the decisions and controls the environment—the child, or his parents and other adults. Children who are allowed to develop some sense of competence in the world grow up with an "inner locus of control." They see control as being within themselves and feel they have power over and responsibility for what happens to them. Others who see control as outside themselves (who have an "outer locus of control") feel helpless and impotent.

If a child doesn't recognize that certain behaviors win approval and rewards while others lead to punishment or disapproval, he doesn't develop a feeling of control over his environment. The rewards and punishments seem to be random and are more related to the parents' whims or moods than to his behavior. When he grows up, he doesn't feel in control of his fate, but feels like a victim—at the mercy of others. In addition, parents who don't feel a sense of control within themselves communicate this lack to their children and make them feel insecure. Children who identify with such parents develop an outer locus of control, too.

Parents need to maintain a balance between controlling children when necessary while still remaining responsive to the children's need to feel a sense of control over their environment.

SENSE OF IDENTITY

Another difficulty that besets many IAs is confusion about who they are and what they want from life. People who have not successfully resolved their "identity crisis" literally don't know what is important to them.

How Does a Weak Sense of Identity Affect Relationships?

Difficulty with commitments.

Those who have not come to terms with their identity have conflicts over basic values concerning such things as money and possessions, their career choices, or what they want in their mates. As a result, they are unable to plan for the future and have difficulty making commitments to others.

These people often respond to their lack of goals with an excessive desire to play rather than work. They are reluctant to settle down and make compromises in their life styles. They tend to live for the moment rather than plan for the future, and they seem irresponsible to others. Having little tolerance for frustration, they always insist on doing what they want. For example, if their mate is going through a difficult time, they say they don't want "the hassles." The Fun Seeker and the Perfectionist often exhibit this behavior.

Overly past-oriented.
Conflicts over identity keep some people overly rooted in the past, since they don't think they have much of a future. They may want things to be like the good old days when they didn't have much responsibility and others did the worrying for them. Either they become Devoted Sons or Daughters and stay overly attached to their parents, or they carry their expectations into their current relationships, relying on their mates to take over where their parents left off.

Strong fears of being controlled.
People who are not yet sure of their identity are vulnerable to fears of losing themselves in their partners. They don't always know how they feel about things, since they haven't yet worked out their own values and beliefs. These people are generally attracted to others who appear to know exactly what they want. Although they may feel more secure with such people, they also feel more threatened by them. As a result, they frequently create distance to protect themselves.

Overly controlling behavior.
Some who haven't yet worked out their identity problems try to hide their conflicts and insecurities from themselves by acting certain about everything. They give themselves away because they make an issue over everything and act much like teenagers (and, incidentally, two-year-olds) who have to defiantly go against any-

thing their mate proposes. The Defiant Disagreer is the best example of this type.

Overly Strong Sense of Identity

Some people appear to have an overly strong sense of identity. Their career choices or their ideas about relationships seem never to have been in question, even when they were children or adolescents. They always knew what they wanted to be when they grew up. Although these people may seem enviable to others who've had to struggle to find themselves, they too can have trouble later in life.

Often these overly sure people haven't developed their own sense of identity but instead swallowed whole what their parents wanted for them (or, conversely, did exactly the opposite). They are usually very compliant and have parents who are very strong-willed and controlling. As a result, they don't question their parents' judgment and never learn to make life choices for themselves.

Their beliefs are often rigid as are their expectations of themselves and their mates. They are traditional in orientation and expect their relationships to be just like their parents'.

Sometimes these people begin to change and grow in their thirties or forties. They go through a period of questioning and may make drastic changes, frequently discarding even the good in their lives.

Why Do People Have Difficulty Working Out Their Identity?

Our sense of identity is an integration of all of our childhood identifications. Young children imitate their parents, taking their identity from them. When they become adolescents and young adults they add identifications and experiences from others—teachers, other family members, friends, the media. They then build on this foundation to form their own sense of identity, figuring out what is important to them and how they want to see themselves.

"Finding yourself," as it is frequently called, is usually a difficult process, beset with much conflict and confusion. In our society, with its frequently changing norms, values, and expectations, it has become a tremendous struggle for people to decide what they want for themselves as well as what they expect in their mates. To complicate matters further, many people are handicapped by parents who gave them mixed messages.

If parents have high expectations of their children's level of achievement but are also critical and unsupportive, the children grow up feeling incapable of meeting parental expectations but powerless to reject them. Frequently, this results in their inability to decide what they want to do with their lives. They are afraid to try and perhaps fail at careers that would please their parents (and their own ideals), but they can't quite accept anything they consider less.

Sometimes people can't decide what they want for themselves because of conflicts regarding identifications with their parents. For example, if a man was successful as a professional but was very weak and inadequate at home, his son, not wanting to be like him, may reject the whole picture, including the professional success. The son might not do this consciously; rather, he can't decide what career he wants or he is unable to "find himself."

Children might also reject as role models parents who are belittled and devalued by their spouses—as, for example, when a boy's father is dominated by his mother, or a girl's mother is dominated by her father. Studies show that identification is strongest if the child perceives the parents' marriage as egalitarian.

PROBLEMS WITH SELF-ESTEEM are typical in Intimacy Avoiders of all types. When low self-esteem is combined with overdependency it leads to behaviors such as we see in the Constant Clinger, Passive Procrastinator, People Pleaser, and Martyr. These people feel needy and incapable and handle it in various ways.

Some are vulnerable to criticism and become Sensitive Sulkers or depressed Clingers. Others become overpossessive and perhaps Jealous Doubters.

If someone lacks self-esteem but feels less dependent on a relationship, he may devalue and avoid getting involved with others. Perfectionists, Romanticists, and Narcissists follow this pattern.

On the other hand, some IAs strongly defend against their feelings of low self-esteem, becoming Constant Critics, Workaholics, or Mr. Machos, for example.

Those who can't "find themselves"—can't work out their identity—also create barriers to intimacy. Because of their inability to know what they want, they commonly avoid commitments. Many of these people are overly fearful of being pushed in the wrong direction by mates and consequently keep their distance. They are also more likely to cling to their past and stay too involved with their parents or children from a previous marriage. Not knowing where their future lies, they are reluctant to give up old ties.

In all of these situations, low self-esteem or lack of identity causes greater vulnerability to avoidance of intimacy.

10

Current Changes In Relationships

CHANGES IN ROLES

While there has been a greater emphasis in recent years on intimacy in relationships, it is paradoxical that other changes in society have made intimate relating more difficult to negotiate than ever before.

The single most important change is that most women today no longer stay home after marriage or after having children. In greater and greater numbers, they are choosing to continue with their careers. While this change is no doubt necessary and desirable, since it offers greater freedom of choice for both men and women, it also presents problems of adjustment. Long-established roles and expectations have to be modified, but it is difficult for most people to adjust their roles and redefine their values without experiencing some conflicts. While conscious expectations of oneself and one's partners are more easily modified, unconscious ones frequently remain the same. The most liberated men and women still have remnants of traditional roles imbedded in their unconscious, even as they play out their modern roles. Contradiction and conflict in messages and behavior are the results.

Effect on Women

In the past, the major role for women was to support men and children—emotionally and physically. Now women want to be able to develop themselves and become all they can be. Yet they can't give up feelings of guilt that they are not there primarily to support their children and husbands. They were raised to see themselves as the force behind the family, not persons in their own right. As a result, women who have outside jobs or careers frequently retain most of the responsibilities in the home. They often feel that although they have careers, their "real" jobs are still taking care of the home and children.

These women are given mixed messages. While encouraged to develop themselves and their careers, at the same time they have been programmed to feel responsible for others. When they try to "have it all," they frequently feel overwhelmed and overloaded. They want more help from their husbands. They want men to give them what women have been giving men for years —emotional support and help at home.

Unfortunately, the husbands frequently don't know what to do—or that there is anything to do. Rather than giving support to others, their primary goal was to develop themselves to their full potential. They have what women need more of—the thrust toward self-development and independence of functioning. But they have always depended on women to perform the helping, maintenance, and supportive functions, taking care of details at home and giving them emotional sustenance.

Very often the functions that women perform are invisible. Like air, they are only noticed when missing. This probably explains why women, even professional and executive women, still do 70 percent of the housework as opposed to men's 13 percent. (The rest is done by hired help.) While working women do less than women without outside jobs (they do 83 percent), it is still not an equitable division of labor. Yet most men with working wives feel that they do a great deal, and compared to the past— what most of them are used to and saw when they were growing up—they are right. But in order to be comparable to women, they have a long way to go.

Most of the time, men don't know what chores they should

be doing. Their ideas of what needs to be done are different from most women's. This is also true with regard to emotional support. Men frequently don't understand what their mates want when they ask for emotional support and communication. Their concepts of listening, giving empathic responses, or being emotionally available are different from those of their wives. Part of this is related to their different views of intimacy (explained more in Chapter 11 on Intimacy) and to different styles of communication (explained in greater detail in Chapter 14 on Communicating).

Many who have written on this subject say that these differences won't go away until men raise children. Then sons will have a nurturing father with whom to identify. Although this would certainly help, we also have to change the way women act toward their children. Women must learn to treat their sons and their daughters more similarly. They must expect personal growth from their daughters as well as nurturing, and supportiveness from their sons as well as personal development.

Some women are greatly conflicted about working outside the home after marriage. Although they may want to have the freedom that earning their own living brings, many of them are very much afraid of giving up their dependent position. Or they may doubt their ability to succeed in the business or professional world. They strive to be independent, but because of their fears and feelings of inadequacy, they may yearn for the option of not taking a job or not considering money when accepting a job. As a result they may give mixed messages to their mates, wanting and expecting more independence but being upset when they get it.

Women who choose to keep their jobs after they have children frequently feel conflicted and guilt-ridden. Many women feel compelled to work because of social pressures, their own and their husbands' expectations, or financial demands. The greater emphasis on materialism in our culture, as well as the higher cost of living (which frequently necessitates two incomes in a family), has also obliged many women to work outside the home.

Some of these women say they would prefer to stay home, but still want the money and the freedom their careers provide. They may demonstrate their conflicts over working, even when they aren't aware of them, by spending money (buying a new house or car or remodelling), thereby making their jobs necessary, and at the same time, expressing anger at their spouses for not supporting them while they have young children at home.

Effect on Men

Men have mixed feelings about their women working outside the home, too. More and more of them expect their wives to help carry the financial burdens, and many feel that working women are more interesting and better companions. In spite of this, some men have difficulty handling the consequences of their wives' careers.

Recent studies indicate that many of them suffer loss of self-esteem and depression. Dr. Graham Staines and his colleagues at Rutgers University found that men whose wives worked were less satisfied with both their jobs and their lives in general than men whose wives were home. This was true for all men regardless of their jobs or income level.

Dr. Ronald Kessler and Dr. James McRae Jr., of the University of Michigan, found that while married women who were employed had better mental health than homemakers, their husbands tended to have lower self-esteem and to be more depressed than the husbands of housewives.

Although neither study indicated that the majority of husbands feel this way, they do alert us to a fairly prevalent problem. Why do so many men feel less happy and less satisfied with themselves and their lives when their wives work?

One possible source of unhappiness for these men is the decrease in emotional support they may receive. Traditionally, women have been the major emotional support of the family. When they are also working, they don't have as much time or energy to devote to their husbands and their problems. Many men feel psychologically abandoned when women leave the home to pursue careers and jobs. They have counted on the "mother of the family" always being there with a hot meal ready for them when they get home. These men may not even carry a key to the house, clearly demonstrating their expectation that "mommy" will always be home waiting for them.

When wives work they are are less dependent on husbands for their own self-esteem, as well as less attentive to their husbands' needs and problems. The men may suffer from feeling that they are second in their wives' lives.

Husbands are often even more disturbed when their wives work while there are young infants and children at home. Many of them want their wives to be home with the children, but also feel the financial pinch of having to totally support the family themselves.

Also, some men are dissatisfied when their wives work because they feel they are failures as providers and, by extension, as "men." This is particularly true when wives work out of economic necessity, and in our current economy this is true of practically all working women. Most men in their mid-thirties and older were raised with the expectation that they would completely support their families. Most women getting married today expect to share the financial burdens with their husbands and, in return, expect the men to share household chores and provide emotional support. Yet the unconscious images these men have of themselves still rest on their perceptions of their success as "good providers." When they have to share that responsibility with their wives, they may feel like failures.

When the man is the sole financial provider, he often uses his financial power to get the upper hand in the relationship. At the very least, he may have control of the major spending. When the wife works, his power and control are diminished. This shift of power frightens many men who depended upon it to maintain their image of themselves. They feel stripped of an important source of potency. Sometimes they are also inwardly frightened that if their wives become too independent financially, they will leave them. They fallaciously believe that their wives need them only for financial support.

Another problem that men encounter is women's desire that they be more open with feelings and emotions. Men who for all their lives have been trained to hold in their feelings, to keep a "stiff upper lip," are now asked to be open and honest about their fears, hopes, and insecurities. But many men are not in touch with their feelings. Years of suppressing feelings and hiding them even from themselves take their toll and make it difficult for them to switch gears. Moreover, they often hesitate to be open because they are unsure or frightened of the consequences of showing their true feelings. Even though the rules seem to have changed, and they are told it is no longer considered feminine to cry or be sensitive, many men still feel deep down that expressing tender feelings makes them less strong. Emotions and unconscious feelings and expectations simply cannot keep up with intellectual acceptance of ideas.

Not only are men confused about this issue: regardless of what they may espouse, many women still expect their men to be as strong as their fathers were (or as strong as they wanted their fathers to be). Although wanting openness and sensitivity in their men, they are often not prepared for their mates' fears and insecurities. So instead of praising their partners for sharing their feelings, these women sometimes become disappointed and angry with them for not being strong enough.

THE NEW INDIVIDUALISM

In the last decade, people's values have changed from the complete sexual freedom of the seventies to a revived desire for committed monogamous relationships. The last few years have also seen a different type of individualism and self-development. There is a new emphasis on materialism and status seeking, and on self-improvement—for both men and women. More people than ever are involved in personal fitness, personal comfort, and personal growth. And, while there is basically nothing wrong with that, many young people with strong desires for "excellence" and for high levels of achievement have difficulty integrating their personal goals and values with those that foster closeness. As a result, each person in a relationship concentrates primarily on his own development, whether personal or work related, and nobody is "minding the store." Each one is expecting support from the other.

In addition, there is often competition between partners. In the past, partners could be competitive about their children's affections or their social popularity. Now they compete in their success at work, with each partner trying to be at least as successful as the other. A partner who is lacking in self-esteem might not feel genuine pride or satisfaction in the other's achievements but instead may see them as a threat. If partners are in the same or a related field, the competition can be worse, since their accomplishments can be directly compared.

Materialism

There has been a gross overvaluation of material wealth in recent times, so much so that respect and regard are awarded on the basis of financial success. This is also affecting our intimate relationships.

Many people base their self-respect and self-esteem on their monetary worth. Some (primarily women) choose mates on the basis of financial success rather than other qualities that might make intimate relating easier. Others spend an inordinate amount of time and energy trying to be financially successful, to the detriment of their relationships.

This has always been true for some men. Now it is also true for many women. The old stereotypes about men and women in relationships are no longer valid—it is no longer true that women seek intimacy and commitment and men avoid them. There are more and more women whose major focus is on their career. Intent on achieving success, and feeling that they have to work harder than men to do so, these women frequently invest too much time and energy in working. They are becoming Workaholics, sometimes outdoing their mates and colleagues in the process.

Also, because they no longer need men for financial security or for their self-esteem, more women than ever are avoiding serious relationships. Since they function more independently, they do not have to seek intimacy-at-any-cost. In addition, many career women are fearful of losing their hard-won independence and freedom in a relationship. Afraid of becoming dependent and submissive, as their mothers may have been, these women may evade commitment completely. Many become Perfectionists—hiding behind traditionally male ploys of being very choosy—or select other ways of distancing.

Shifting Gears

A related problem is the difficulty many people have in shifting between attitudes required at work and those necessary for intimate relationships. Business transactions frequently demand placing their own interests first, no matter what the consequences to others. In order to be successful in the workplace, they have to be competitive. Even in the professions, aggressiveness is often most rewarded with material success and status. That this attitude prevails at work is understandable. But it is all too frequently applied to personal relating as well. As a result, some people see relationships as nothing more than transactions in which they try to make the best "deal"—by attempting to give as little as possible to their partners and get as much as possible for themselves.

Self-Interest Above All

The media contribute to this type of transactional thinking by depicting people as being nice to others only because of guilt, fear, and other negative emotions. One might come to the conclusion that being giving, kind, and considerate is neurotic or certainly self-defeating. Popularized versions of humanistic psychologies and assertiveness training all encourage people to watch out for themselves.

Encouraging people to stand up for their rights and not be manipulated by others is certainly useful. When people feel manipulated and controlled by unrealistic parental or societal expectations, they need to learn to be more "selfish." However, when applied to intimate relationships, this attitude can be misinterpreted to mean that we do not have to compromise or otherwise conform our behavior to others.

Another danger with this attitude is its assumption that the overwhelming majority are people pleasers, who need encouragement to watch out for their own interests and assert their own needs. This is not true for everyone—or even for every woman—as some writers have suggested. Moreover, this approach is not likely to be adopted by overcompliant people, since they would be afraid of the consequences. Finally, merely advising people to be more assertive, or more in touch with what they want, is hardly enough to make them change their entire orientation and style of functioning.

This "looking out for yourself" attitude is more likely to be adopted by those who already fear others will take advantage of them. It can then be used to justify self-protective behavior. Because most of these people would rather not have to adjust to others, it is very convenient for them to get on the self-interest bandwagon and adopt that style of relating. You can often hear them say, "I don't want to have to compromise or give up what's important to me." They would rather believe one shouldn't have to make adjustments to others—that all should flow naturally. If these people are uncertain about whether to risk giving and loving, this belief makes them feel more sure they had better not.

What does all this do to intimacy and close relationships? It certainly does not help them. While there are many individual reasons for insatiable needs or unrealistic expectations, the current societal values encourage these expectations also.

Removing the Veils

Becoming a True Intimate

11

Why Intimacy?

How important is intimacy to our well-being? Do women want it while men try to avoid it? Psychologists and psychiatrists from a wide variety of theoretical backgrounds all agree that intimate involvements are crucial for everyone's mental health and satisfaction.

Freud's idea of mental health includes the full development of the capacity to love. For Freud, love is very much tied up with sexual satisfaction. Although he felt that the sexual desire was transformed into affection and caring by "sublimation" (a "defense" that substitutes "higher" level satisfactions for more basic ones such as sex or aggression), for him sex was still the basis of love.

Dr. W. Ronald D. Fairbain, an early founder of the object-relations movement (a variant of the psychoanalytic movement), felt that intimacy was a primary need. He said that the newborn's earliest, deepest wish is for a satisfying, loving connection with a nurturing mother. Object-relations theorists consider that connection to be more important than satisfaction of instinctual sexual drives.

Erich Fromm, a neo-Freudian psychoanalyst, said that in average adults there is a great longing for the security and rootedness that they found with their mothers. Fromm believed that people are very much aware of aloneness and separateness from others, and wish for union. He felt that the need to escape from separateness and isolation is so strong that many people are willing to renounce themselves to be part of another. These people transcend separateness and experience their identity by becoming part of somebody bigger and more powerful than themselves. Other people overcome isolation by having power over others through domination. In both these situations, the people involved lose their integrity and freedom, living on and from each other.

Erik Erikson, who formulated a model of the stages of lifelong development, saw intimacy as an essential part of our psychological growth. One of his stages focuses on the major life crisis in the development of intimacy.

Psychiatrist Harry Stack Sullivan postulated the need for love, which he defined as an intimate exchange with a fellow being, as one of the three basic needs. He said that this need was often intertwined with the other two basic needs: for security—feelings of self-esteem and personal worth—and for sexual satisfaction. Sullivan believed that loneliness is more terrible to experience than anxiety and that people seek companionship even when they become intensely anxious in the process.

Surveys of college students, older men, and the general public have suggested that, for both men and women, interpersonal intimacy is a deep source of life satisfaction. The most common problem reported by readers of *Psychology Today* is loneliness. Most people said they look to their intimate lives for their deepest satisfactions and for relief from loneliness.

In a recent study, Dr. Daniel McAdams, a psychologist at Loyola University of Chicago, found that there is an increasing emphasis on the importance of personal intimacy to the individual's sense of fulfillment. While he found that women report a greater need for closeness than men do, the difference is very slight. In addition, since men are not brought up to think intimacy is important to them, they may need it as much but not consciously admit their need to themselves or be willing to report it to others. In therapy, men often come to recognize just how necessary close interactions are to their well-being.

DIFFERENCES BETWEEN MEN AND WOMEN IN EXPRESSION OF INTIMACY

Men and women define and express intimacy differently, as Ted Huston, a psychologist at the University of Texas at Austin, has found. Women want to talk things over, especially the relationship, while men prefer to spend time enjoying activities together. Men feel close in sharing the pleasure of their mates' company.

Many psychologists, such as Kathleen White at Boston University, Kate Gilligan at Harvard, and Lillian Rubin, a psychologist and author of *Intimate Strangers*, say that the differences in how they view intimacy reflect deeper differences between men and women regarding need for autonomy versus need for closeness. Males learn independence and autonomy as they grow up; females learn how to make close connections. Traditionally, the risk for men has been too much closeness, which might threaten their autonomy, while for women the risk has been too much separation, which might make them fear abandonment and aloneness.

Another difference between the sexes is that men are not raised to believe that their personal interactions should enhance others' development. Women, on the other hand, are raised to support others' growth—even over their own.

Each partner can be enriched by learning from the other and taking on the other's strengths. However, neither can change to be like the other. Rather, both partners need to accommodate the other's perspectives.

Dr. McAdams's study also found that intimacy serves different functions for men and women. For women, a close relationship leads to greater happiness and satisfaction in the relationship itself. For men an intimate relationship carries over into other areas of functioning. It affects their inner sense of security and certainty about the world, giving them greater confidence to achieve more. They are more insulated from stress at work and show greater adaptability and strength. Although intimacy also serves to bolster women's emotional strength and confidence, the survey didn't show that it affects them this way as much as it does men.

Women have traditionally defined themselves in terms of their close relationships, while men have defined themselves in terms of their work-related achievements. Although positive experiences of intimacy may give both men and women an inner feeling of satisfaction and serve as a buffer against stress, they may each describe their subjective experiences differently. This may be a result of different emphases in their lives at the time of the study and may change as more women become achievement-oriented in the world.

WHAT IS INTIMACY?

According to Erich Fromm, in *The Art of Loving*, love means making a commitment without receiving guarantees, giving yourself completely in the hope that your love will produce love in the beloved. It is an act of faith. Fromm believed that in order to love, you need the courage to take the risk, to accept the possible pain and disappointment. For him, love is giving—the highest act of potency, the act that makes you feel strength, wealth, power. But many people see giving as impoverishment. Infantile love is "I love you because I need you." Mature love is "I need you because I love you." Lovers feel others' needs as their own.

Harry Stack Sullivan said that love exists only when the beloved assumes virtually equal importance to the self in all areas. Instead of doing for the other to get what the doer wants, the person who loves does for the other to contribute to the other's happiness or to support the prestige and self-esteem of the beloved. This feeling of sensitivity to the other person is the beginning of a "we."

How can we distinguish true intimacy from the illusion? How do we know when we have it? Sometimes it seems easier to recognize in others than in ourselves. When we see people who seem to need only each other, we consider them intimate. When we see people who are affectionate and sexually close, we say that they are intimate. Are these people truly intimate? That depends on how you choose to define intimacy. There are many kinds of closeness, but only one type provides the gratification that most of us are looking for. The basic elements of a mature intimate relationship are described below.

Closeness Between Two People

Any relationship of closeness—emotional or physical—can be called intimate. Even temporary relationships, if they are close, are intimate to some extent. However, what most people want involves more than temporary closeness.

Feelings of Affection and Love

One of the most important things we want from others is love. We need to feel affectionate, warm feelings toward the other person and to have these feelings returned. We want to know that the other cares about us and wants to be with us. Physical closeness without caring is essentially ungratifying.

A Special Type of Giving

People give to each other for many reasons. Not infrequently they give because they want something in return, or because they are afraid to say no. When people are in a loving relationship, they give to each other out of caring for the other's welfare. They give freely, with joy in giving. They don't keep track of how much they have given. That is because they trust the other to give back.

Cooperation and Interdependence

People who are close usually cooperate with one another in work and in play. There is a sense of compromise and consideration for the other person. Each person in an intimate relationship depends on the other to some extent. It is a mutual interdependence rather than a lopsided dependency in which one leans more heavily than the other. Although the intimates feel they need each other, they do not need each other in order to live; they merely live better together.

Sense of Commitment

Very often, people who are intimate spend a great deal of time together. They often live together and sometimes get married and have a family together. There is usually a sense of commitment and security between them. While people can be intimate without a sense of commitment, most would feel insecure and unfulfilled.

Sharing of Feelings and Thoughts

An intimate involvement usually means sharing personal feelings and thoughts with each other. True intimates share plans for the future and their deepest hopes, dreams, and fears. There is an openness and trust between them that allows for disclosure of inner feelings.

Combination of Individuality and Union

No matter how close intimates become, they should never lose their essential separateness. They should continue to think for themselves, feel for themselves, and act by themselves. Each person's integrity must be retained. Mature intimate relationships are a unique combination of union and individuality in which each person can function independently and cooperatively at the same time.

Equality of Power

There are three major ways of relating to others: being subservient to them, domineering of them, or equal to them. Of the three, the third is the most difficult. Yet it is the only one in which both people can maintain their integrity and freedom and still have closeness and intimacy. Submissive-domineering relationships are symbiotic in that each lives off the other. In some relationships of this kind, such as those involving Tyrants or Mr. Machos, the dominant partners are tyrannical and unresponsive to their mates' needs. However, as with the Rescuer and the Workaholic, sometimes dominant partners are protective and giving to their mates. In either case, the situation is not one of equality. These relationships may satisfy many people's needs for a long time. However, in a mature love relationship, the balance of power should be as equal as possible.

Is there no power or influence in an equal relationship? Are the partners totally free to do what they want? Of course not!

When you relate closely and cooperatively with someone, you have to relinquish total freedom. You have duties and responsibilities to your partner, as he or she has to you. However, when you have a strong sense of autonomy and integrity, you do not have to fear being controlled. You have the ability to maintain your self-respect while accepting the need to give to or do for others. The influence that one person has on the other is based on affection and respect rather than fear and coercion.

WHAT DOES A GOOD RELATIONSHIP INVOLVE?

What are the personal ingredients that contribute to intimacy? If you can learn what you need to achieve intimacy and where you or your partner is lacking, then you can work on specific problems and dramatically increase the intimacy in your relationship. Here are the specific abilities that you need in a relationship.

Ability to Care for Another

The most important element in achieving intimacy is the ability to care for another person. You have to be able to allow another person to become important to you. This makes you vulnerable to them, so to venture caring for someone else, you must be willing to trust them. You must also feel strong enough to survive rejection, should it occur.

Ability to Tolerate Closeness

Intimate relationships also require the ability to tolerate closeness. Many people—because of their fears of merging, control, trust, depletion, and so forth—are not able to be emotionally close to another without great discomfort.

Ability and Willingness to Communicate With Others

In order to maintain intimacy, you must communicate with your mate. You must be willing to share your deepest feelings and thoughts, even when they are not popular. You should openly express positive feelings and desires as well as disappointments in the relationship. In order to feel free to do this you have to feel able to trust your mate to respect your confidences and not use them against you.

Ability to Give Freely

Giving freely to your mate is another essential ingredient in a relationship. This means doing things for your partner as well as giving in material ways. You must be able to consider others' needs, not just your own. That means willingness to compromise and give up what you want at times, without resentment. When each partner in a relationship is considerate and giving to the other, intimacy flourishes.

Ability to Assert Your Own Needs

To have a complete relationship, you must be able to assert your own needs. You need to be in touch with what you want and to communicate your feelings. But in order to do that you must also be able to risk the rejection that might come as a result of your assertiveness, and you must risk having your needs or wishes refused. Nevertheless, unless you can assert your own needs, you cannot feel good about giving or being close to anyone. Part of assertiveness is being able to say "no" and set limits with your mate. Here, too, you must be willing to risk rejection. You must have good judgment about what is reasonable to give and what is reasonable to expect. This is often the major problem preventing people from asserting their own needs.

PERSONAL CHARACTERISTICS NEEDED FOR INTIMACY

What personality characteristics will enable someone to care, give freely, and carry out all the other requirements of intimacy?

Emotional and Functional Independence

An important element of healthy intimacy is independent functioning and thinking. Although some interdependence between partners is necessary, overdependence presents tremendous barriers to closeness.

Why should independence be such a vital and necessary ingredient in intimate relationships? As I discussed in greater detail in Chapter 8, overdependency can cause problems in relating. Independence allows you to freely give to your mate and to compromise. Your giving becomes genuine, not grounded in fear, because you are less vulnerable to fears of abandonment and rejection.

When you are more independent and therefore less needy, you are free to develop better judgment about people. You can learn whom to trust and whom not to trust. You do not have to be unduly afraid of being cheated, nor do you have to let yourself be taken advantage of in order to get your needs met. You can finally be free.

An added advantage is that when you are not preoccupied with getting your own needs met, you can feel free to be empathic to others. You can understand different viewpoints and behaviors in terms of the other person's needs, ideals, and beliefs. This not only facilitates giving to the other person, it also allows you to maintain perspective and saves you a great deal of unnecessary hurt. When you cannot see things in the context of others' needs and feelings, it is easy to interpret everything in terms of whether they love you or not. When you begin to see that others have needs or priorities to attend to that may have nothing to do with you, you will not take personally every refusal or rejection of your wishes. You will be able to see that their behavior is not related to whether they love you or care about you.

Sense of Self-Esteem

A healthy dose of self-esteem is another very important ingredient in intimacy. You need to feel good about yourself because of your own efforts and characteristics, not because of your mate's praise or support. This involves being able to reward yourself for your own achievements. While another's recognition is rewarding, it should not be necessary. If you are not dependent on others' approval, then you are less frightened of their disapproval and you are less vulnerable to fears of criticism, control, and rejection.

This makes it possible to be an equal partner in an intimate relationship.

Current research by Arlene Skolnick, a psychologist at the University of California, Berkeley, suggests that marital satisfaction for both men and women is strongly related to self-confidence. Not feeling either victimized or inadequate is very important in promoting happiness in a relationship. She found that self-esteem in one partner positively affects both.

Self-Love

Feeling good about yourself, even loving yourself, is very desirable in intimate relationships. Yet many people are suspicious of those who "love themselves too much" because of their confusion between the concepts of "self-love" and "selfishness." People are not supposed to be selfish and think only of themselves. Society considers that wrong and even sinful. Many people are also taught that it is immoral to love themselves, the theory being that if they love themselves too much there will not be any love left for anyone else.

Self-love and selfishness are not the same thing at all. In fact they are opposites. Loving yourself means valuing yourself as a person—considering yourself someone of worth. Instead of making you more selfish (interested only in yourself), it makes you less selfish and more able to love others. Truly selfish persons do not think enough of themselves—do not love themselves enough. They cannot give love because they feel they need it all for themselves. They should not be thought of as immoral and sinful. They should be helped to love themselves so that they can love others.

If you don't love yourself, you tend to disbelieve other people's love for you. You doubt others' motives in giving to you. Self-love and self-acceptance enable you to freely ask for what you need and accept what loved ones give at face value. You are not forced to deny your own needs, or cover up your fears, hopes, and desires with compensatory strivings. Self-love also makes it easier for you to give to others because you are not chronically envious of others and resentful of what they have.

Sense of Identity

It is very important to maintain your own integrity and identity in a relationship. In order to do this you have to have your own "center." That does not mean being self-centered—thinking the world revolves around you and expecting others to meet your needs. Having your own center means that you know who you are, what you stand for, and what feelings and thoughts are yours. It means you understand your needs and your reactions to these needs.

When you have your own center you are less likely to become confused between your own values, ideas, and feelings and those expressed by your mate. This protects you from the fear of losing yourself in or being taken over by another person. Your center also helps you lose your fear of being controlled: you know what you want and what you are willing to do for another person. You are more confident in your judgment and in general less frightened of being close.

Maturity

All together, the personal characteristics needed for an intimate relationship create a picture of mature, emotionally and functionally independent persons who have a firm sense of themselves and good feelings about themselves.

Not surprisingly, this picture is borne out by research. A recent update of a long-term study of marital satisfaction by E. Lowell Kelly of the University of Michigan and James J. Conley, a Connecticut psychologist, showed that marital satisfaction is negatively related to neuroticism in both sexes.

You may be convinced by now that all of these emotional factors are desirable and help make relating easier. But how can you achieve them?

With the help of Chapter 12 you can begin by examining your unrealistic expectations of people and relationships. Then, by following the steps in Chapter 13, you can start the process of overcoming your own barriers to intimacy. The later chapters will help you learn to communicate better and deal with your IA mate.

12

Demystifying Myths of Intimacy

We have many underlying beliefs about relationships and how they should be. Some of these beliefs are rooted in our instincts; others are rooted in our early childhood development. They are encouraged by western culture through advertising, movies, TV, and romance novels.

Many of these romanticized notions are not consciously expressed, but they operate below the surface to undermine relationships and make people feel unloved and unsuccessful. What are the ten most common of these myths?

1. Falling in love is forever.

Falling in love is wonderful. It is a combination of fantasy, passion, and obsession. You are sexually attracted to someone and attribute all kinds of wonderful qualities to him. You feel instantly close and comfortable, as if the two of you were made in heaven for each another. All at once you drop barriers and share your innermost thoughts and feelings—and it feels right. Because of the excitement of the moment, other aspects of your lives are temporarily put aside. Your lover gives you all his attention and you pay full attention to him. You feel euphoric and believe this is the most important thing in your life.

What does falling in love actually mean? Psychoanalysts say that falling in love is an unconscious transference of feelings from your childhood loves—your parents—to someone who reminds you of them. When you meet your love, there is an unconscious recognition of familiarity. There must be some truth to this, or else how can you explain your instant attachment and feelings of closeness? Why do you find your beloved so easy to trust? After all, you don't really know this stranger to whom you've readily given your heart.

The intensity of falling in love is increased by the immediacy of the situation. The combination of familiarity and novelty makes for tremendous sexual desire. In addition, there is the totality of the experience—you both put aside everything else. Another factor, which adds to the passion, is the insecurity involved in a new relationship. The anticipation and the lack of predictability cause a great deal of tension, which is experienced as excitement.

Some relationships continuously stimulate this excitement because of their stormy or otherwise insecure nature; at least one of the partners is always kept guessing. The price for this is usually too high, however. What is gained in excitement is lost in security and true intimacy.

Being in love, as opposed to loving someone, cannot last in a predictable, secure relationship. While partners can continue to feel sexually attracted to each other, the novelty and profuse excitement soon wear off. Everyday life has a way of making even the most romantic encounters dull. When people fall in love, they tend to exaggerate their similarities and disguise their differences, but after lovers get to know each other better, their fantasies have to give way to more realistic assessments. When they discover their incompatibilities, they are often disappointed. They are left with deciding whether they enjoy each other's company and can interact in a mutually satisfying way on a daily basis.

Research on the nature of love by Dr. Robert Sternberg, a Yale psychologist, confirms our observation that passion develops most quickly and fades most quickly in a relationship. In the couples he studied, passion declined to a plateau and remained there as other aspects of love developed.

2. Love is all that matters; therefore it should be enough to make you happy.

One of our most basic instincts is love. Our early lives depend on it, and when, as adults, we don't have someone to love, that seems like the only thing that matters. We believe if only we had love, we would be happy. The media tell us that love is all-important—through romantic novels, movies, and innumerable popular songs. Commercials tell us that if we wear the right deodorant or drink the right cola, we will get love and everlasting happiness. It is easy for us to overestimate the power of love in a relationship.

Unfortunately, once we settle down and accept the relationship, other things once again regain their normal importance. While we all want and need love, we also require other things—work, family, friends, recreation. By assuming that we should be happy if we are in love, we make life and relating even more difficult than they have to be.

While you may not expect love to be enough to make you happy, you may believe that being in love is all that is needed to make a marriage happy. This is also a myth. Romantic love is wonderful, but a marriage needs more to flourish. In addition to having passionate feelings and the unconscious attractions that we call "falling in love," a couple has to genuinely respect one another, be capable of giving each other emotional support, and enjoy sharing daily life together. This is what psychologists call "mature love."

Research on what makes marriages happy was conducted in 1985 by Jeanette Lauer and Robert Lauer of the United States International University in San Diego, California. They surveyed 351 couples (300 reportedly happy) married 15 years or more. The reason most frequently given for their marital success was seeing one's partner as one's best friend and liking him or her "as a person." The second most frequent was belief in marriage as a long-term commitment. Also high on the list were agreement about aims and goals in life and a desire to make the marriage succeed.

3. People in love almost merge, become one.

People have an unconscious desire to merge, to be one as mother and child are one. For the brief period of falling in love and during brief intense moments thereafter, two people can be so close as to feel that they have merged emotionally. Sexual intercourse—the ultimate act of love—symbolizes this merging. Many people feel that in marriage their needs and those of their partners are one.

Society has perpetuated this view, expecting women to take their husbands' name. Until World War II, when women began to enter the work force in great numbers, the couple functioned as a unit. Women couldn't survive on their own and therefore couldn't see themselves as separate. Only recently have women been able to even consider maintaining their own name after marriage.

Although it is tempting to believe that we become one when in love, it is not possible—partners' needs cannot mesh all the time. Even if it were possible to merge with another, it would not be comfortable or healthy, for we would fear being submerged and losing our identity.

People need to be separate, to maintain their own identity. If you have so much togetherness that you risk losing yourself in your mate, you may eventually feel smothered.

True love allows you to be yourself, to have your own interests, ideas, likes, and dislikes. In order to be close to each other, you don't have to enjoy all the same things or do everything together. The more you develop your individuality, the more you have to bring to your relationship. Sharing individual interests, such as jazz or racquetball, can enrich both of your lives, adding greater depth to your relationship.

As Erich Fromm explains, in *The Art of Loving,*

> In contrast to symbiotic union, mature love is a union under the condition of preserving one's integrity, one's individuality. Love is an active power in man; a power which breaks through the walls which separate man from his fellow men, which unites him with the others; love makes him overcome the sense of isolation and separateness, yet it permits him to be himself, to retain his integrity. In love the paradox occurs that two beings become one and yet remain two.

A variant of the merging myth is "You should be so open and honest with your partner that you can share your every thought and doubt." This leads to the unfortunate situation in which partners share their fleeting sexual fantasies (of sleeping with others, for example) or tell their partners their "true" feelings about in-laws or a child from a previous marriage.

While these disclosures may be made in the name of honesty, they often produce pain. It serves no positive purpose for your partner to hear about your innermost fantasies; most likely they will cause your mate to feel threatened or inadequate. Describing your "true" feelings about someone close to your mate can also be detrimental—to your mate and to your relationship—for it places your partner in the impossible predicament of having to defend family members or joining in their betrayal.

This myth also leads to confessions of infidelity, which the erring partners feel would be wrong to keep secret from their mate. By disclosing the behavior to their spouses, the transgressors may reduce their guilt, but they do so at the expense of their mates, the victims of the injustice. That only compounds the injustice done. Discretion and tact are necessary to prevent unnecessary hurt, even in the closest of relationships.

4. When people marry, they should be prepared to sever all ties to others—family and friends—for their loved ones.

During the marriage ceremony, you promise to "forsake all others." Your commitment to each other comes first. That doesn't mean, however, you must abandon everyone else in your life. Most of us understand this to mean that we should forsake previous lovers, not that we should exclude the possibility of all other relationships in our lives.

You must, of course, consider your spouse's needs for attention and companionship. But it is unfair for either spouse to demand so much time that relationships with parents, friends, or children from previous marriages suffer.

Family and friends enhance your marriage by providing warmth, support, and social contacts. It would be a tremendous burden for a person to be the one and only in another's life and have to meet all of the partner's emotional needs.

The amount of time you spend with others will vary with

the circumstances. Since you may not always agree on what is desirable, you'll need to discuss your feelings and concerns and compromise with each other.

Some of you may fear that your partner will not have enough time, energy, or love for both you and others, and that you will be shortchanged. If you can see the advantages in maintaining other relationships and recognize that, with compromises, your spouse can give you enough and still have time for others, it will be easier to accept sharing.

5. In a good relationship, partners give each other what they need without ever having to be asked.

When you were an infant, your mother responded to your every need without being asked. Some of you carry into your relationships this fantasy of having your needs met automatically. You may feel that your partner should know you well enough to know what you like and what you want—for your birthday, for dinner, and in bed. Sometimes your partner does. But even in the best of relationships, you may not get what you hoped for. Partners can't read each other's minds. Mothers know what infants want because their needs are so basic. Adults' needs are much more variable and individual.

Some people hint at what they want by giving it to their mates; they make a fuss about their spouses' birthdays because that's what they themselves would enjoy. Others hint with offhand comments about preferences in clothes or a show they want to see. Unfortunately, hints are not always understood.

Instead of interpreting your mate's ignorance of your desires as lack of caring, or vaguely hinting at what you want, sit down together and discuss the things that are important to you. You might say, for example, that for your anniversary you would enjoy a romantic dinner more than a surprise party, or that you prefer personal rather than household gifts for Christmas.

6. Partners can never ask too much of each other.

Another way to state this myth is "If he loved me, he would do what I want."

While parents are called upon to sacrifice their own needs and desires for their children, it is not reasonable to expect this from your mate. While you can rightly expect a great deal—even temporary sacrifices—there is a limit.

Many of you believe that a partner who loves you will change to accommodate you, especially when you believe the partner is in the wrong. Unfortunately, your partner's abilities may interfere with what you want. For example, you may expect your mate to calm down, overcome fears, become more ambitious or more outgoing. Perhaps you expect your mate to lose weight or give up smoking or drinking. In spite of a well-intentioned promise to change, frequently your mate can't follow through. When you see no change, you may interpret it as lack of love or as not wanting to be with you enough. Sometimes you may think the remedy is to withhold sex, affection, or a commitment, hoping your mate will want it enough to change. This is bound to fail and to cause resentment and hurt on both sides.

The simple truth is, you may be expecting too much. Love and will power are not enough to change deeply ingrained behavior. Although it is sometimes difficult to accept limitations in your partner, recognizing them and realizing that they don't signify lack of love can lessen your disappointment.

Your partner may not be able to do what you want because of needs or interests that conflict with yours. People sometimes mistakenly interpret their spouses' behavior as a reaction to them. If their husbands or wives work late, they believe they don't care enough to come home. If their partners don't go along with their wishes, they see it as evidence of lack of love. In both instances, the partners are probably fulfilling their own needs.

Men often feel that if they get a better job offer out of town, there should be no question about moving. If their wives object, because of their own jobs or other commitments, the husbands interpret the objection as lack of love or loyalty. Today, unlike the past when couples' financial and social interests depended solely upon the man's livelihood, what is in a couple's best interest is not always clear. Even when the couple operates as a unit economically, the partners' needs are not identical. As separate people, each with individual needs—for their own jobs, their own friends—they can't always do what their partner asks. The more they see themselves as capable, independent people, the less they will need their partners to always do what they want.

7. Marriage partners are responsible for each other's happiness.

Those who feel responsible for others (because of parental dependence on them in their youth) and those who feel that they can't provide their own happiness (because of feelings of powerlessness and helplessness) are particularly susceptible to this myth.

Hollywood and fairy tales have perpetuated the notion of Prince Charming rescuing Cinderella and living happily ever after. Single men are led to believe that the "love of a good woman" will ensure their happiness. This is not real life. When you have found your "savior" but are still unhappy, you may place the blame on your mate's behavior. And when she is unhappy, you may blame your own actions.

Lovers want to make their beloved happy. But no matter how much they try, they can't always succeed. Marriage is only one part of your life. Other aspects, such as your career and interests, are also important and have power to make you feel fulfilled. Even if you're delighted with your partner, you might not be content with your job, your relationship with your family, or yourself. You need to find happiness within yourself, which comes from developing your own sense of identity and self-esteem.

A related myth is "Your partner should help you to be all you want to be." Partners often expect their mates to help them change. They want them to encourage their growth and development, helping them to become more successful or overcome their problems. In other words, they make their spouses responsible for them. When they don't grow or develop the way they want to, they blame their mates. Just as you can't get your mate to change for you (see myth 6), you can't expect your mate to be responsible for you. Often people with these two mistaken notions marry and blame each other for their own lack of change or growth.

8. Lovers should put their beloveds before themselves.

While we would all like our lovers to put us ahead of them, as our mothers did when we were infants, this is not a reasonable expectation. We may sometimes sacrifice for our loved ones, and certainly put their real needs before our whims, but we can't do this all the time. During times of crisis or sickness, we often have to forgo our own desires to help our mates, and we may have to give up some pleasures at times as a compromise. But for one lover to place the beloved ahead of self all the time is masochism. Those who feel they regularly have to relinquish their own needs to keep their mates' love (like the Martyr) don't sacrifice willingly, but do so out of fear of abandonment. They eventually resent their mates and often make them feel guilty because of their own privation.

9. Love should be unconditional.

A common wish is to be taken care of and given to without anything expected of us in return. Unfortunately, however, everything comes with a price tag. When our mates give to us, it is with the implicit expectation of the return of our love and appreciation. When the relationship is unbalanced and one partner gives more than the other, the giver frequently demands control. The husband who takes good financial care of the family usually wants final say on spending. The woman who does all the cooking and cleanup decides on menus and the schedule of meals. Expecting to get without giving is unrealistic and bound to lead to disappointment.

Just as we may feel we should be given to without strings, we may feel we should be loved no matter what we do. Again, this is totally unreasonable. We are expecting our partner to accept us no matter what the physical or emotional cost. People who have such expectations frequently test their mates by provoking them or asking a great deal of them as proof of their love. They suspect anything that their partner gets out of the relationship. While love involves a great deal of tolerance of the beloved's idiosyncrasies, it cannot be unconditional.

10. Marriage partners shouldn't have to work at a relationship—it should be easy.

Everywhere we look we see people fall in love and live happily ever after. Ads, TV, and movies all make it seem so easy. When they first meet and fall in love, everything is easy. Nothing matters except being together, and they may temporarily put other commitments aside. If, once married, they continue to believe that their relationship will be effortless, they will see having to compromise as a sign that their marriage is deteriorating.

Unfortunately, life can't continue like the courtship or honeymoon. While initially it may have been easy for partners to put other things and people aside to be with their beloved, in the long haul this becomes more difficult. People must go back to their other responsibilities of work, family, and friends. At first, couples find it easy to put their mate's needs first; it is not important what they do as long as they are together. That too becomes more difficult after a while, as other issues become important: where they go, what they eat, who does what in the house, and so on. Building a life together involves many decisions—how to spend money, how to allocate time, and, later, how to raise children. It isn't possible for partners to always agree. Unless they discuss and work out differences, they'll have many conflicts and resentments.

Howard Markman, a psychologist at the University of Denver, conducted a study of 26 couples seen before marriage and five and a half years after. The best predictor of their marital satisfaction was their ability to talk to each other and work out problems. This was more important than how happy they were before marriage.

The Lauers' study of happily married couples (previously cited) also indicates that the willingness to work things out when there are difficulties is vital to the success of long-term marriages.

To ensure a long, happy marriage, you must continually work at it. This involves telling each other how you feel—what is important to you and what you want and need from each other. You must listen to your spouse and try to see his or her viewpoint, and you may need to compromise with each other on some issues. While your needs may not always be compatible, working out the conflicts together is the key to lasting satisfaction in your marriage.

13

Overcoming Your Own Barriers to Intimacy

The first step in overcoming your own barriers to intimacy is to recognize what they are—are they huge barricades or merely thin veils? You can begin by evaluating your patterns of relating. Are they similar to any of the IA types described in earlier chapters? Although few of you will fit any one type exactly, you may find certain elements of them familiar. By seeing how these IAs act, and comparing yourself to them, you can get some clues about how you come across to others and why they react to you as they do.

If any of the IAs' fears or problems pertain to you, try to look underneath your behavior to understand what feelings motivate you. If you are honest with yourself, avoiding defensiveness as much as possible, you can recognize the fears, needs, or vulnerabilities that cause you problems in relationships.

Since most of us are not in touch with these feelings and often erect complicated defenses to protect against fears and feelings of vulnerabilities, facing your feelings can be difficult. However, with practice, you can learn to be more aware of the underlying emotions that influence you.

Look for signs of conflict and repressed feelings, such as indecisiveness, vague feelings of discomfort, depression, anxiety, inability to act, difficulty concentrating, forgetfulness, sleeplessness, and restlessness. Other indications of problems are overreactions to others or to situations, or constant anger. If any of these appear persistently, there's a good chance that you are in conflict and consistently pushing down your feelings.

You can discover your unconscious emotions by consciously focusing on what you are experiencing at different times—when you try to control your anger, when you choose not to express it, when you cover up your fears or anxiety. Other clues to your feelings are slips of the tongue, dreams, body language, and facial expressions.

If you feel your main difficulties involve continually choosing IAs, you will need to understand why you do this. How did you react to previous mates? Did you usually find they were too withholding, too controlling, too critical? How do you react when people close to you are critical? Examine any patterns in your choice of mate as well as your behavior with them that might point to similar difficulties with each.

Scrutinize your current needs, fears, and disappointments. After reading these chapters on Intimacy and Myths of Intimacy, try to determine how much of your dissatisfaction is due to having chosen the wrong mate and how much is due to your unreasonable demands and needs. When you find yourself feeling hurt and deprived, decide whether these feelings come from your mate's denial of love or come from within yourself. Remember that you may not really need so much approval, reassurance, or attention but feel you do because of your insecurity. You may need to keep reminding yourself that you feel hurt because of your unrealistic expectations and not because you are truly being rebuffed.

The next step is to understand why you feel as you do. From the explanations in earlier chapters, you can see that much of your behavior is determined by your early experiences. Try to discover how your feelings and ways of interacting with others are related to how you felt as a child and how you were treated as a child. How many of your present-day reactions to your spouse or lover were programmed when you were a child? Examine how your expectations of your partner and of the behavior you are willing to accept from him and may even encourage, are related to your family background.

Many patterns of behavior develop by identifying with parents; others are reactions to the way children were treated by parents. Look at your family now. How do they operate, with you and with each other? This is a good way to see how some of your patterns developed. For example, in a family where the parents are impulsive and childlike, one of the children is usually chosen to be the "strong one," or caretaker, while another may be allowed to be the "baby" and remain like the parents. The children assume these roles partly because of their inherent qualities and partly because of their parents' expectations of them.

Sometimes when people recognize their parents' contributions to their problems, they use them as an excuse for continuing their behavior—after all, it isn't their fault. They blame their parents as they may have blamed their partners in the past. Just because you recognize that your current problems are largely attributable to past problems with parents, you don't have to spend your life blaming and resenting them. You don't have to try to change your parents or believe they have to change for you to feel differently. However, you do have to change your behavior toward them. You have to first understand why you react as you do to your parents—and to mates—and STOP THE REACTION.

As an adult your behavior is your responsibility, and you, above all, pay the consequences if it is dysfunctional. If your behavior avoids or sabotages closeness in your relationships, blaming your parents or your spouse will not change it. Only YOU can change it.

All of us have to accept at one time or another that our parents weren't all we would have liked them to be. For the lucky few with reasonably good parents, this may be easier to accept. But none of us has had perfect parents. They all lacked something and they all erred somewhat in our upbringing. When you accept that they didn't give you everything you feel you should have had as a child, AND NEVER WILL, you are on your way to emotional health and maturity. When you accept that your spouse WILL NOT and CANNOT make up to you what you did not get, and that that is OK, you will be farther along on the road to true intimacy.

You do not have to rework your conflicts with your parents to master them. You do not have to make up now for what you didn't get then. You are an adult and no longer have those needs. Somehow you managed to survive, and often thrive, without them.

First you must learn to accept your feelings as your responsibility—not your mate's, not your parents'. Once you really understand your parents and why they behaved the way they did, you can stop feeling that you were inadequate, helpless, bad, or unlovable. Knowing why you feel like a "terrible person" and that this feeling isn't realistic allows you to stop reacting as if you are one.

Remind yourself, whenever you begin to react to these feelings, that you are really reacting to your father or mother. Your reaction is that of a helpless child who couldn't protect himself, or had to have everything done for him. Now, as an adult, you are no longer in that same helpless predicament and no longer have to react as you did.

Remember June, the Constant Critic? She was able to recognize that her strongly critical reactions to her husband and children were directly related to the way her mother treated her. She had to be perfect in everything she did, to court her withholding mother's approval. She found she was reacting to herself and her family as her mother did to her. In order to become less critical and more accepting of her husband and herself, she had to keep reminding herself that her anxiety every time things at home weren't perfect was due to her fear of not pleasing Mom.

In the sections that follow, I have provided concrete suggestions to help you overcome some specific problems.

SELF-LOVE AND SELF-ACCEPTANCE

Begin by accepting yourself as you are.
If you want to change, then, paradoxically, you must first accept yourself for what you are. Feeling sorry for yourself or being angry with yourself is self-destructive. If you spend your time and energy feeling angry or guilty because you do not like what you see in yourself, then you will have no energy left to do anything about it. Instead you will wallow in self-pity, blame, hurt, and anger.

Learn to give to yourself.
Be good to yourself. Take care of yourself physically and emotionally. If you don't, you cannot be good to anyone else. Feed yourself emotionally so that you do not need others to feed you. Only you can meet your own needs completely. You are no longer

a helpless child who needs to be taken care of by mommy. Now you can be your own "mommy" and pamper and feed yourself. Set your own limits with others, and consider your own desires and your own best interests. Sometimes this may be accomplished by giving to others, but never do so at the expense of yourself.

If you begin to give to yourself, you will feel less needy, and paradoxically, others will tend to give you more. A mate who feels less pressured by your demands can feel freer to give to you.

Not feeling as needy allows you to be more giving and less afraid of depletion, which in turn encourages others to give to you also. In addition, when you are less needy, you do not need others to be perfect—you can accept them as ordinary human beings. You are less angry with them. They sense this greater acceptance and can be more giving with you.

Being able to give to yourself allows you to develop the ability to wait. You begin to realize that if you do not get your needs met as soon as you would like, or at all, the world will not come to an end—you do not disappear, you survive. Anxiety and desperation about your needs and wants makes you a slave to others and to yourself. If you do not react to every frustration with despair and feelings of deprivation, you can have greater freedom of action.

Carol, the young woman who fears depletion, was for a long time unwilling to give to herself. Even though she was quite capable, she felt angry at having to take care of herself. She strongly believed that she could feel loved and secure only if someone else supported her financially and did things for her. With therapy, she has begun to take the risk of doing for herself—making herself happy. To her surprise, she likes it. And feeling less needy and more able to focus on her partners has improved her relationships dramatically.

OVERCOMING OVERDEPENDENCY AND FEAR OF ABANDONMENT

Don't confuse emotional needs with the need for others to take care of you.

There are two types of dependency—emotional and instrumental. Emotional dependency is the need for affection, contact, and approval from others. A certain amount of it is absolutely necessary for attachment and love to be present. Instrumental dependency, on the other hand, is the need for help in doing things, in taking care of yourself. The two are often confused in people's minds.

Try to understand how you became excessively dependent.
In order to overcome too much of any kind of dependency, you must first try to understand why you are afraid of being independent. For this, you will have to explore your childhood. Your early relationships provided the basis for your feelings of insecurity, your fears about being on your own, and your reluctance to take care of yourself. Look at your early relationship with your parents and their relationship with each other. Sometimes looking at your current relationship with them helps you to see how it must have been when you were small.

Although you can't rewrite the past, and understanding your childhood and your parents doesn't automatically change anything, seeing the roots of your difficulties will help you. People often feel guilty about being dependent and deny it. If you understand the reasons for your dependency, it becomes easier to accept. You will see why you feel the way you do and why you have fears and internalized bad feelings about yourself.

Liz, the Fickle Lover, feared being rejected and abandoned. She was afraid to trust any one man to be there for her. At first Liz had difficulty accepting fear as the reason that she could not choose one man. Most people are reluctant to admit that fear and insecurity motivate their behavior, and like Liz, they have elaborate disguises to hide their fears. However, only after you see what your fears are and why you have them can you hope to overcome them. Liz's realization that she never felt accepted by her mother, and that this was her mother's problem and not proof of inadequacies in herself, had a freeing influence on her.

Examine what keeps you dependent.
People often don't take the risk of developing greater independence because of what they fear they'll lose—their mate's love or

approval, for example. They feel their mate, or perhaps their parents, needs them to stay dependent and encourages their incompetence to keep them attached.

It is likely that if you have been overdependent, your mate unconsciously prefers it that way, even if complaining a great deal. Your growth would upset the balance of power in your relationship and probably make some waves.

When Barbara (in Chapter 5) offered to help with the budget, at first her husband Arthur resisted. "If she knew how much money there was left at the end of the month, she would spend it." She realized that he was threatened by her gaining any control over the spending. Although he more easily justified his right to make all the decisions before she was working, he still wanted full control after she got a job. He was threatened by any attempts on her part to assume responsibility because it meant that he was inadequate as a *man*.

Barbara persisted in confronting Arthur with his behavior and showed him how it was contradictory. He finally accepted her contributions to decisions about money and other areas of their life such as going on vacations. He said he wanted more of a helpmate, and he got one. Eventually, Barbara and Arthur worked out a new relationship on a more equal level.

In this case, as in many others, a partner readjusted to the situation and the relationship improved. But this doesn't always happen. If your partner is very much invested in your dependency, and can't change gears, you may be in for much renegotiation and even battling. In some cases, you may even have to recognize that your partner will never willingly accept the changes.

Another thing that may keep you dependent is the meaning you give to working and supporting yourself. For example, Barbara was reluctant to get a job for many years, even after her children were teenagers, because she was convinced that contributing to her own support would prove she wasn't as good as the other women in her neighborhood who could spend their time shopping and going to the spa. She believed that only a professional job or her own business would make her feel good about working. Before she could feel comfortable seeking work, she needed to examine these feelings and work them out.

Try to avoid interactions with mates that repeat your parents' patterns of encouraging dependencies.
Unconsciously you tend to repeat the patterns set up in your childhood unless you are aware of them and consciously avoid them. If you are not married or involved, take the risk and try a different kind of mate. The experience may seem strange to you at first because the mate is so different from what you are used to, but this mate may be just what you need.

If you are already involved, you can change the way you and your mate interact. By refusing to become entangled in the pattern of being the child and having your mate take care of you, you can induce him to treat you differently.

Work on developing the conviction that you can take care of yourself.
Knowing you can take care of yourself places you in a position of strength, not weakness. Being prepared to fend for yourself helps you to be less afraid of others' reactions. Being less vulnerable to others gives you greater confidence in dealing with them.

Practice doing things independently a little at a time. Independent behavior comes in little steps, not all at once. Many people hesitate to take the first step because they are afraid of falling on their face. If it is a little step, so what? You can pick yourself up. Children would never walk if they were afraid to take that first step. Try to encourage yourself and take little steps toward doing for yourself and thinking for yourself. Successes in this area can be euphoric.

When Gayle (our Tyrant) recognized the need to become more independent, she was frightened at first. She needed Ray to do her bidding because she felt unable to take care of herself (and her children). So, with support, she started out gradually, first taking a part-time job near her home. Once she felt more comfortable working, and when her youngest child began school full-time, she looked for jobs that involved more responsibility and longer hours. At home she also took on a larger role, assuming more of the budgeting responsibilities. Her confidence in herself grew as she did more and more.

OVERCOMING THE NEUROTIC NEED FOR APPROVAL

First try to understand why you need constant approval from those around you.

Our Status Seeker Arlene discovered why she constantly needed to win approbation and recognition from colleagues, neighbors, and everyone else around her. She was able to trace her feelings to a childhood in which she was never accepted for what she was but always had to meet the family's needs. Because her family's love was so conditional on her performing for them and pleasing them, she expected everyone else's love to be like that. She could never feel accepted unless everyone lauded her achievements.

Once she saw the reasons for her feelings, she could work on developing other ways of feeling good about herself and allow her personal rat race to be ended.

Overcome the myth of universal acceptance.

Most of us realize that nobody can be loved, approved of, and accepted by *everyone*—or even by one person—*all the time*. Yet that is what we sometimes expect—either social approval by all with whom we interact, or approval by our partner of all we do in our relationship. Some people go so far as to want and need approval from people whom they do not like or respect. If you do not think well of people, then why do you need their approval? If their judgment is poor, then their approval is not worth having. Yet some people feel hurt and put down when even a person unimportant to them doesn't love or approve of them. They give the power of judgment to everyone and anyone and thus take it away from themselves. They make the assumption that others' opinion of them is always right. Basing your self-worth on pleasing another is at best a tenuous situation. You have to remember that others' thoughts and feelings, about you and about everything, come from their needs and do not make for an objective, unbiased assessment.

Learn that others—even authorities—are not gods.
Other people, in whom you invest so much power to judge you, are merely *people*. They are as fallible as you are. Learn when you need expert advice and when you can judge for yourself. You do not always need to consult with everyone else.

Distinguish between disapproval of your behavior and rejection of you.
When others do not approve of your behavior in a specific instance or criticize a piece of work that you have done, do not assume that they do not like or approve of *you*. The person that you are far surpasses one instance of your behavior or work. Even if others do not approve of one of your personality traits or characteristics, they have not encompassed all of you.

Don't give others the ability to manipulate you.
Needing others' approval all of the time allows them to manipulate you. You always feel that you have to please them. Do not allow others to manipulate you into giving to them out of a need to keep their love or approval. This merely backfires, setting up resentment and leading to less real giving and loving. On the other hand, do not be afraid to give for fear that you will not have enough left for yourself. Giving does not deplete, it makes you feel richer for giving—*if* you give because you want to, not because you feel that you have to.

Develop your own internal sources of judgment and approval.
Learn to trust your own judgment and to give yourself approval. No amount of reassurance from others can substitute for the self-confidence you get from real achievement. If you did not get this feeling from being on your own before marriage or when growing up, you have to develop it now.

OVERCOMING FEAR OF MERGING

Try to find your own "center."
The fear of merging with another person is the fear of no longer experiencing yourself as separate from your partner. When you

don't know if what you are doing or saying reflects your own thoughts and feelings or those of your partner, then you are having difficulties in individuation. To combat them, you must develop a sense of yourself as unique. You must learn to recognize what *you* feel, what *you* stand for, and what *you* need. When your feelings, thoughts, and opinions are coming from yourself and are not merely reactions to others, you will have your own "center."

Andy (in Chapter 7), who feared merging, found that in order to allay his anxieties about being close to his wife, he would have to develop a stronger sense of himself as a separate person. In therapy, he explored his own feelings, values, and beliefs. When he felt good enough about himself to risk standing alone, he was more able to be close to his wife without feeling threatened.

Set your own priorities.
Separate your needs from those of your partner. Decide what is important to you in your relationship, in your work, and in yourself. Do not allow your partner's needs and desires to infringe upon your decisions about what you want. That does not mean that you never compromise or give up what you want for another; it merely means that when you do, you are aware of it and do it willingly.

Work on your ability to disagree with your partner.
If you are not afraid to displease your partner, then you can risk disagreement. Then your partner can't control your actions or your feelings. You must recognize your tendency to discount your feelings when they put you in conflict with your mate. You must fight against this subtle control that you bring on yourself. You can do this by always asking yourself, "What do I really want to do, regardless of what my partner wants?"

OVERCOMING FEAR OF BEING CONTROLLED

Do not give to others out of fear.
Giving to those you love should always be out of free choice. You might give because you want to share with your partner, or because you want something in return. But you should never give because you feel intimidated or coerced in any way. This only

leads to resentment and feelings of being controlled, and will ultimately destroy the intimacy in the relationship.

Recognize that you always have a choice when someone requests something, even when it sounds like a demand.
People who fear being controlled usually feel that their loved one's request is their command. They may respond to it with either compliance or rebellion, but always with anger and resentment, expressed or not. It is important to recognize that even the most demanding partner is not your boss or your parent. Remember that people can control you only if you allow them to. You are the one who gives others the power to control you, and you can take that power back. You can choose to make the ultimate decision of what you do or give. If you feel intimidated by your partner, you must not give in. The less you respond to intimidation, the more others respect you. You do not have to acquiesce. Learn that you possess a great power, the power to say "no."

If your mate's requests make you angry, ask yourself, "Why does this threaten me?"
Perhaps you feel that if you do not comply your mate won't love you or won't give to you. Is this reality or is it merely your own fears? If in fact your mate does withdraw, withhold love, or get angry—so what? How long does it last? What happens afterward?

People often feel more free to give when they feel free not to give.
When you no longer fear being controlled, you can do for others without feeling compromised or forced.

Before Mel, the Perfectionist, could choose one woman to marry, he had to overcome (at least to some extent) his fear of being controlled. First, however, he had to acknowledge it. After stripping away his defensive explanations for his lack of commitment, he was able to see that he feared a woman might dominate and rule him.

Part of Mel's problem was that he anticipated being controlled and so never gave anyone a chance; the other part was that he was attracted to women who, like his mother, were strong, overbearing, and controlling.

Although he needed to question his choices of women, he also had to give them a chance. He had to realize that since he was no longer a child who couldn't say no to mommy, he did not have to allow himself to be dominated. As he felt less threatened, he became more able to get attached to a woman and give to her without fearing total loss of autonomy.

OVERCOMING FEAR OF CRITICISM

Learn to listen to the other person's complaints without reacting.
When people complain to each other, frequently what they want is merely understanding of their feelings. They want their partners to hear them out, acknowledge their hurt, and show concern. If you are too defensive about being criticized, you can't be sensitive to others' feelings and needs.

Recognize that you are your own worst critic.
If you fear criticism, you are likely to interpret others' comments as worse than they are meant to be. Recognize that your partner is probably not criticizing you as harshly as you believe. When your mate makes unfavorable comments about you, it doesn't mean you are "no good" and unworthy of love.

Do not assume that your partner's criticism of you is necessarily right.
Your partner could be misinterpreting you or blaming you for something that is not your fault. Sometimes listening carefully before reacting will clarify this situation without hurt and anger.

If you did something wrong, admit it.
If you know you are at fault, apologize and try not to repeat your mistakes. Certainly, if you don't feel justly criticized, you can say so. But hear out the criticism first. You may not be aware that you've hurt your mate. Although the situation might appear to be minor, it is helpful to avoid becoming defensive and to try to see your mate's viewpoint. Rather than focus on the accusations, try

to understand the hurt feelings. By reassurance that you care about your partner and meant no harm, you will be furthering your intimacy rather than creating a barrier. Even if your partner is misinterpreting your behavior, reassurance will be more advantageous to both of you than getting angry over a wrong accusation. You might be overinterpreting the comments and your mate could be wrongly reading you.

John, whose fears of intimacy were described in Chapter 7, finally overcame his problem. After becoming aware that his automatic, defensive overreactions to criticism were interfering with his relationship, he was determined to learn to counteract them. He recognized that as soon as his wife said anything that wasn't clearly positive, he became self-protective. He began to realize that much of the problem was in his interpretation of what she said. He was more critical of himself than she could ever be, because of his lack of self-esteem. When he no longer interpreted her complaints as a total "put down" of him, he was able to feel less threatened. Then he could really listen to what she was saying. He was soon able to distinguish between her general frustration and her discontent with his behavior, and learned to evaluate what she really wanted from him. As a result of this change, and his work on building his self-esteem, his marriage improved enormously.

OVERCOMING THE FEAR OF TRUSTING

Distinguish between those whom you can trust and those whom you cannot.

People who fear trusting have usually been hurt in the past because of having trusted the wrong people. "Gut reactions" won't tell you very much—in fact they will often mislead you. The first rule is: don't trust anyone too soon. It is just as foolish to trust everyone as it is to trust no one. Learn to distinguish between those you can trust and those you cannot. Ask yourself, "What do I really know about them?" Observe their behavior in different situations, with you and with others. As the relationship grows, you will be able to see them under more and more varied circumstances. By looking at their past behavior you can anticipate their future behavior.

Remember that trust is not all-or-nothing.
Determine the conditions under which you can trust others. Recognize that different people can be trusted under different circumstances and with different things. For example, you might be able to trust your mate to be responsible but not to always be sensitive to your needs.

In addition to different types of trust, there are varying degrees of trust that are appropriate for particular types of relationships or for one time or another. Trust develops in stages. As you gain greater intimacy, you can and should expect more and more from your mate, who will also expect more and more from you. If you expect too much too soon, and let your expectations be known, your partner may feel overwhelmed or angry.

Build trust gradually.
The way to build trust in a relationship is by giving other people a chance and then watching what they do. Test them with small amounts of trust first, in areas that most concern you. Then you can see if you want to trust them with more.

Evaluate your expectations.
When you have difficulty trusting others and anticipate betrayal, it often takes great effort from your partner to reassure you. To appease your fears, you may be placing unreasonable demands on your mate. Even in the most intimate of relationships, some requirements are too much. If you're creating that situation, nobody will ever come through for you to the extent you feel you need. (See Chapter 12, "Demystifying Myths of Intimacy.") The danger here is that your partner will either become resentful or you will always be disappointed, which will reinforce your fears that you can't count on anyone.

Karen, the Jealous Doubter, had to overcome her inherent distrust in men in order to improve her relationship with her husband. She had to examine her own unrealistic negative expectations (learned from her mother) that all men are unfaithful. They had caused her to be overpossessive and suspicious. Since she expected her husband to be unfaithful, she interpreted any time away from her as disloyalty. When she recognized that she was expecting too much from him and began to allow him some leeway before becoming suspicious, he became less resentful of her and more able to compromise.

Take a risk: give others a chance.

If you want greater intimacy, then you have to take the risk of investing your feelings. You must give others a chance and not back off too quickly the first time you are disappointed. You won't find perfect people who will never disappoint you. You must allow others room for mistakes and room for their own needs.

14

Reaching Out Through Better Communication

STYLES OF COMMUNICATING

Women complain that their men don't talk to them, don't listen to them, and don't understand them. Men gripe that women talk too much, are too frivolous in what they talk about, and are too emotional in their conversations. How true are these attitudes?

Basically, there are many differences in the way men and women communicate and in how they use conversation. They often have misunderstandings in their everyday encounters because of these differences.

Deborah Tannen has reported extensive research in her book on miscommunication, *That's Not What I Meant.* In discussing differences in how men and women communicate, she points out that men focus on the message; women, on the emotional meanings (the metamessage). She says that, in general, men believe that the only important aspect of communication is the information transmitted. This can cause problems in everyday communications between couples because women use talking to maintain emotional contact, which men tend to interpret as unnecessary and frivolous.

They also differ in what they want to talk about. Men are more interested in objects and events, while women prefer people and relationships. Men often say that they would like to discuss politics, news events, or sports but their mates would rather talk about other people or their own relationship.

Women often think that men who are silent during a conversation aren't listening to them. However, this too may be due to a difference in style. Women tend to make more listening noises ("uh-huh," "mhm") than men do. Some men show interest by challenging what a woman says; others just say nothing.

Because of their general problem-solving attitude, many men respond to a woman's complaints by suggesting changes rather than by acknowledging her feelings. Frequently the woman just wants a sympathetic ear.

Another important difference among people's communication styles is the degree of directness. This varies with personality, but in general, men tend to be more direct than women. Women try to avoid confrontation, thinking that the avoidance will protect them from feeling too hurt if they don't get what they want. They also avoid hurting others, by not being too "honest"; for example, they do not tell others directly that they don't want to see them or don't like how they look.

Because of their indirectness, women are more sensitive to subtleties of expression. They are hurt when men don't pick up messages that they send, and they may read meanings into what the men are saying. This may explain why women expect men to know what they like and want. A woman may think, "How come I know what he likes and he doesn't know what I like?" The answer is that men are not usually as sensitive to these subtleties of communication.

Since men are less attuned than women to messages of involvement, husbands are often not aware of metamessages that their wives are expressing. Wives' feelings may be hurt because their husbands don't give the same meanings to conversations as they do.

Husbands don't necessarily ask how their wives feel or how their day was. Most men say, "She'll tell me if she wants to." But women interpret this to mean that men don't care.

When interpreting metamessages (emotional undertones of communications) you may pick up signals that weren't intentionally sent out. Or you may misunderstand messages because of fears that predispose you to look for criticism, rejection, or control. You may also misinterpret others because your preconceptions of how they feel or what they think prevent you from hearing them.

Men and women can have difficulties communicating because of style differences that are unrelated to gender. People vary in how fast they talk and in whether they have long or short pauses between thoughts. A faster talker who takes fewer and shorter pauses will dominate the conversation, and the other people will feel unable to get a word in edgewise.

People also differ in other aspects of communication: whether they cut into others' conversation; their degree of loudness and ways of expressing emotion; whether they respond to others' conversation by asking questions; and whether they express agreement or remain neutral.

WHAT CAN YOU DO ABOUT THESE CONFLICTS?

Try to understand your own and your partner's style of communicating. Pay attention to your pauses, your rate of speaking, your loudness, and your tone. Notice especially how direct you are and how you may be conveying underlying messages. If you realize that you are indirect or give underlying messages that you may not consciously mean to give, try to recognize why. Are you indirect as a response to others—your partner, or someone from your childhood? Indirectness often reflects fear of directly expressing yourself and a wish to please.

It is helpful to recognize that one or both of you may be misunderstanding the other. You may be picking up the wrong emotional message (metamessage) or even misinterpreting the tone or words used. If you assume, in advance, that your reaction may not be what your partner intended, you will be willing to check with your mate to make sure you understood or to believe the line, "I didn't mean what you thought I meant." You are less likely to feel hurt and more open to an explanation.

When a conversation isn't working and you feel you are being misunderstood or don't quite understand your partner, don't keep repeating yourself in the same way. This tends to escalate differences.

What you can do is make small adjustments to the others' conversational signals. For example, if your partner cuts in when you are speaking, make your pauses shorter to indicate that you're not finished. You can overtalk an interruption, raising your hand as if to say, "I'm not quite finished," or you can say, "I'm not finished yet."

If you have been indirect in your approach, you might try becoming more direct and specific. It may also help if you can change gears—your rate, your tone, your level of loudness—to be more congruent with your partner.

The most powerful way to change an interaction is to do so without making it explicit by talking or acting in a different way.

Another technique to improve communication is to tell others how their style of communication affects you. For instance, a woman may tell her mate that she needs more time to express herself fully. He might explain to her that when he chimes in, he doesn't expect her to stop. Or, you might ask your partner to slow down, or to use a lowered voice because the loudness makes you uncomfortable. When either of you makes suggestions, be careful not to blame or criticize but merely state your preferences.

If all else fails, and you believe that whatever you say will be wrong, ask your partner what was expected in response to a comment or question. Although your partner may be taken aback, not realizing that a specific response was expected, this is preferable to getting enmeshed in an angry debate that nobody wins.

RESOLVING CONFLICTS THROUGH BETTER COMMUNICATION

Try to find the best time and place to talk.

Many couples say that they never seem to find the right time or place to communicate. They are too busy or too tired, or there are too many distractions (such as children, parents, or friends). Although time may be a problem for some couples, many others are merely avoiding a confrontation with their mates about the real issues. They may be upset about their relationship, but they are also afraid of the prospect of trying to change it.

Even people who believe they are close are apprehensive about sharing their feelings with their partners. They are just as reluctant to ask their mates to reveal their feelings or explain their behavior.

They may have secrets they can't share for fear of disapproval, criticism, or rejection. They may be afraid their partners will become angry if they complain openly to them. They fear their mates will yell and scream, pull away, or turn the situation around and attack them.

This is especially true of men. Many studies have shown that men tend to overlook problems in a marriage more than their wives do. Dr. Robert Sternberg, a psychologist at Yale, says that his studies show that women tend to see more problems and view their relationships as more troubled than their husbands do. Dr. John Gottman, a psychologist at the University of Illinois who studied both happy and unhappy couples, also says that wives are more sensitive to problems in marriages. Women are generally willing to confront conflicts in their relationships; men are more likely to avoid them. When they disagree, the woman usually wants to resolve the disagreement, believing she will then feel closer to her husband. But the husband wants to avoid a blowup. He sees the conflict as a source of trouble rather than a way of getting close.

The only way to overcome this reluctance is for both partners to learn to communicate in an open, nonthreatening way. Both have to agree to listen to each other and attempt to understand each other without attacking. The first step in this process is to make the time—if necessary, set aside a specific time and place—to talk privately.

Tell your mate how you feel.
Try to talk, to explain how a behavior or an attitude makes you feel. Emphasize your feelings rather than your mate's transgressions. When you highlight your feelings and play down perceived faults, it allows empathy for you to develop even if your mate doesn't agree with you. You can say that even if you are overreacting or mistaken, you still feel hurt.

Try to remain calm and objective, to keep the offending behavior in perspective. Most of the time both partners are so reactive to each other that it becomes impossible to sort out who is reacting to what.

Avoid blaming and attacking.

Do not blame, accuse, or attack your partner. Avoid character assassination (labels like "childish," "neurotic," or "a tyrant") in the process of complaining about your mate's behavior. Avoid sarcasm as much as possible. Although you may be justifiably angry and you may feel wronged, you will not be productive if you cause your mate to become defensive. Develop non-accusative modes of communicating.

Avoid making yourself right and your mate wrong.

When couples argue, it is rarely with the intent of clarifying the issues and expressing their feelings. They usually want to give each other a piece of their mind and prove that each is right and the other is wrong. Their main thrust is winning their point and having the satisfaction of their mate's admission of guilt and atonement for it.

Even when couples come to therapy together to work things out, frequently they each try to win the therapist over to their position and prove themselves right. If they finally do admit some responsibility for the problem, they were never quite as "bad" or destructive as their partner. And their behavior was always justified, considering what their partner did to them or how upset they were.

These feelings are perfectly understandable and perhaps warranted. However, expressing them vehemently can only serve to alienate your mate and make understanding of your point of view more difficult.

What you want to do is help your mate to give you more time, more consideration, or more caring. If you succeed instead in increasing embarrassment, guilt, or depression, you're unlikely to get a conciliatory response. Your mate is more likely to try to protect against these uncomfortable feelings by denying the validity of your accusations, becoming angry with you for your attack, or withdrawing from you in one way or another. None of these is what you want.

If you present your gripe carefully, in the form of a request rather than an attack, you may see a willingness to try. That is all you can expect.

If you're looking for retribution or compensation, forget it. You might feel you want to hurt, as you have been hurt, and you can do that easily. But then what do you have? Certainly not greater intimacy.

Offer a way out gracefully. Show that you understand how your mate must feel but that it is still important for you to have your needs met.

Be specific about your gripe.
Confine yourself to one issue at a time, and clearly explain what is bothering you about it. If you overload your explanation with grievances, your partner will feel hopeless. Don't just complain about behaviors, no matter how specifically. Request a reasonable change that will relieve the problem.

Make a point of sticking to the current situation rather than bringing up old issues. What happened in the past, although hurtful, is not as important as what is happening now. Neither of you can do anything to change the past. You are not trying to build a case; you want change. Focus on what can be done now. Hurts and grievances should be brought up as soon as possible after they occur rather than allowed to fester and grow worse.

If you are particularly upset about other things in your life, share that fact with your partner. Sometimes you may seem more angry or upset than is warranted, because of other stresses. If that is true, both of you should take that into consideration. Sometimes discussing the situation with your partner is helpful.

Be sure your mate has understood your complaints.
Has your mate understood what you want? You will be surprised at the misconceptions you find. Some of them are due to the way you presented your point (perhaps in your anger and overreaction to the situation you were too harsh or demanding). Other misunderstandings may be caused by defensiveness or fears that you want too much. These conflicts will all have to be clarified.

Don't allow countercomplaints or counterdemands until you are shown understanding and response toward your complaints. Your mate's chance comes when you are through.

Give your partner time to think.
Don't expect or insist upon an immediate apology or admission of guilt. While sometimes, and for some types of people, this will be forthcoming, it often doesn't mean much in terms of real change.

Give your mate a chance to absorb your complaints. Wait a while (sometimes a few days or a week) and observe your partner's behavior to see whether your complaints have made an impact. Often your partner may hear you but cannot give you the response that you want immediately, or may respond internally but show anger and defensiveness at first. Later, there may be more readiness to think about what you said.

What if your mate gets very angry?
That is when you should retreat. Your mate may need to cool off, think things over, or just spend time evaluating some feelings.

Some of you may be afraid to retreat or allow your mate some distance when you are angry with each other. You can't tolerate waiting for a response—you want to know immediately what your mate wants to do. Perhaps you are afraid you won't still be wanted when the situation calms down. If that is the case, your anxious pursuit will certainly not help; it will only drive your mate away faster.

If you become desperate and panic-stricken whenever you have a squabble, you might continue to argue, believing that as long as there is contact, there is hope. This approach tends to backfire, since you are unlikely to come to any reasonable agreements while you are both angry and hurt. At this point neither of you can see the other's viewpoint. Instead, the intensity of your feelings and the destructiveness between you are likely to escalate and become impossible to stop. You might both say things that you later regret, and feel worse in the process. The most effective strategy at times like this is to let it go. Cool off and regain your perspective of the situation.

Learn to listen to your partner.
People have difficulty really listening to each other. They are so busy trying to express their own feelings and getting ready to answer their partner, that they don't hear what is being said. They are too quick to interpret what their partner is saying and too unwilling to actually see things from the other's perspective.

Try to spend time listening even if you believe your partner is being defensive. Are you allowing time for expression of your partner's views, whether you agree with them or not? If you don't understand what they mean, or something can be interpreted more than one way, ask for an explanation before jumping to conclusions about the meaning.

When you believe you understand what your partner has said, restate it, asking whether you interpreted it correctly. If the reply is that you are mistaken, believe it. Don't assume you know better what your mate is thinking and feeling. Give another chance to explain.

This is a very important and overlooked area of communication. Often people believe they "know" how their mates feel and think. When the mates won't admit to being "figured out," they are merely being defensive or covering up. People who assume they "know" could be wrong! They, too, could be defending against their own anger or fears and projecting onto their partners. Even if they are right and their partners are being defensive, a confrontation will only yield alienation. People must be prepared to allow others to explain their feelings in their own way, and to give others the benefit of trusting what is said. If they don't, they might as well not talk to each other at all.

Try to see your mate's viewpoint.
In order to foster communication and intimacy, you must attempt to see things from your partner's perspective, acknowledging the needs, fears, hurts, and disappointments involved. Some of these are related to you and some aren't. But if you want your mate to consider your needs and care about what is important to you, you must do the same.

If you can understand another's viewpoint, you will realize

that the other feels it is the right one. At the very least, the other is likely to feel justified in the behavior and sees no other choices. Do not overreact to these responses. Just listen.

It is important to allow your mate latitude in feelings and reactions to situations. If there is upset or anger with you or with a situation, try to be tolerant even if you don't agree. Your mate has a right to feelings and ideas that may not always coincide with yours—or what you think they "should" be.

Seeing your partner's viewpoint has an additional benefit. It often makes the behavior less threatening. For example, if a woman realizes that her husband is going on so many business trips because of his insecurity and need to prove himself rather than because he doesn't want to spend time with her, it makes the situation easier to deal with. She still may not like it, but she doesn't have to be hurt by it either. Instead of getting angry at him, she might help him to realize that he needn't do this to prove himself. He might be working so hard because he feels that in order to satisfy her he has to make a lot of money. She might reassure him that she would rather have his company than more money (if this is true, of course). Understanding partners' thoughts and feelings can go a long way toward solving problems.

When you understand how your partner views a situation, say so. Make sure you are accurate in your interpretation. Only then can your partner hear you out.

Take the first step in being willing to compromise.

Once you start compromising, and showing a willingness to change your behavior, your mate will be more likely to try to change also. You may not want to change first, but one of you has to begin.

Try to be more tolerant of small things or you will lose your effectiveness when it matters. If you don't make everything a conflict and just fight for the important things, you will have a better chance of being heard. Try to give in on items that are more important to your mate, to offer the chance of giving in on things that are important to you. No immediate response to your efforts? Don't give up. Allow more time.

If you have difficulty communicating directly, try writing your feelings on paper before presenting them.
Sometimes you may need to write things out, either to clarify your own feelings or to help convey them in a nonthreatening manner. Let your mate read your notes, have the chance to mull them over at leisure, and formulate ideas about them. This may seem artificial, but it may work in situations where one or both of you are too upset to express yourselves clearly or listen to the other. Sometimes it helps as a temporary method to stop arguing and listen.

Practice communication.
You and your partner may have to practice communication—listening to each other, attempting to hear things from the other's perspective, and communicating your understanding of the other's viewpoint. This has to be a cooperative effort or it won't work. You must aim toward working out a mutual solution, where each person compromises to some extent.

15

Dealing With
An Intimacy Avoider

HOW TO MAKE THE BEST OF YOUR CHOICE

Realize that everyone has limitations.

Many of you will have difficulty accepting faults in your partner; you may feel threatened because you fear your partner will not be able to give you enough. The more secure you are with yourself and your own ability to take care of your needs, the easier it will be to accept your partner's limitations.

Another reason many of you have difficulty accepting your mate's flaws is that you base your self-worth on your mate's success. When you perceive an undesirable trait in your partner, you may think, "How can I be with a person like this?" You believe your blemished mate is a poor reflection of you—to yourself and the world. It is important to realize, however, that your self-esteem doesn't rest on your mate's achievements and that others don't judge you solely by your mate.

Appreciate the positive aspects of your relationship.

Recognize that some of your partner's faults may have a positive side. For example, if your man spends too much time working (fault), he is likely to be financially successful (positive). And the man who is neglectful about chores and laid back at work, and who doesn't stand up to his secretary or mother (faults), is usually easygoing and tolerant of you as well (positive).

You chose your mate because of your attraction to certain qualities in that person. Often when you are angry about what you see as deficiencies, you overlook the desirable behavior in other areas.

Evaluate your expectations.

Most of us feel that there are certain things we absolutely cannot do without. Often these "needs" cause us difficulties in relationships. They are based on underlying assumptions that we never question.

Unrealistic expectations of partners frequently lead to disappointments. For example, if your father or mother was overindulgent or overprotective, you are likely to expect the same treatment from your spouse because you see yourself as unable to take care of yourself. Your partner, although truly loving, may be unwilling or unable to go along with your expectations.

A woman whose father was very powerful and successful can make her husband feel inadequate if she expects him to live up to her father's image. Other of her father's desirable traits not shared by her husband, such as being handy around the house, having a good sense of humor, or being outgoing, can be unfairly expected from him even though he may have other wonderful qualities that she is overlooking.

Jane was always disappointed with her husband for not being the "handyman" that her father was. Her father always fixed everything that was broken, from the plumbing to her toys. When she saw that her husband was not very handy or interested in repairs, she began to think he wasn't much of a "man." But when she recognized his positive qualities and stopped comparing him to her father, she was much happier in her marriage.

Jane's problem of expecting too much from her husband can be compounded by the overidealized view that some people have of their parents. As children, they may have seen their parents as all-powerful and giving. This image is especially common when a parent is unavailable either emotionally or physically.

You might also have unrealistically negative expectations of your mate. Do you continually expect rejection, criticism, or control, even though your mate doesn't act that way? Examine your own fears and try to deal with the reasons for them rather than transfer blame.

For example, Judy's father was unfaithful to her mother, and everyone in the family knew it. Her mother frequently said that all men were like her husband and passively accepted the situation. Judy grew up believing that all men were deceitful and that she couldn't keep a husband's attention any more than her mother could. Consequently, even though she had no reason to suspect her husband, Joe, she was always worried about his extramarital activities.

Another example is provided by Cathy. Her father left her mother when Cathy was small. Cathy's mother led her to believe that he left because Cathy was "too much trouble." When she became an adult, Cathy realized that marriages break up for many reasons and that her mother blamed her rather than examine the real issues in the breakup of her marriage. Yet Cathy still unconsciously expected her husband to abandon her as her father had. She internalized the feeling that she (and her children) were too much trouble for a man to handle.

Try to discover your underlying assumptions and see if they are true or false. Evaluate exactly what you are expecting from your relationship. You may be relying on your mate to live up to an overindulgent or powerful parent or make up for what you didn't get as a child. If you find you have been unrealistic, it is important to understand why and to change your attitude. In order to achieve intimacy, you must rid yourself of the "shoulds" and "musts" that interfere with accepting and loving your partner.

Give your mate and yourself more latitude.
People vary in the amount of physical and emotional space they need. Even if you both like the same amount of closeness generally, your needs at any one time may vary depending on factors such as work or stress. For instance, some people want to be alone when they are upset about work or feeling sick, while others look to their partners for contact and support at such times. All of these factors need to be taken into consideration when dealing

with your mate. By recognizing that your mate responds to certain situations by either clinging or withdrawing, you can avoid overreacting and causing conflicts.

If your mate is a distancer or a pseudo-intimate If your mate regularly prefers more distance than you do, try to understand and cope with it. Rather than see remoteness as rejection of you, recognize it as a need for greater autonomy.

Since you can't expect your partner to fulfill all your needs for intimacy, seek out friends and family for closeness as well. Often this takes enough pressure off the Distancer so that more responsiveness is possible at other times.

Let your mate know that you want more intimacy. Be sensitive but persistent in your approach. Try to entice rather than criticize. For example, say, "Could we spend time together later this evening? I would really appreciate it." rather than "You're so cold, you never talk to me."

Don't push. Avoid checking constantly to ensure that your mate still cares for you. You'll be avoiding feelings of pressure and a tendency to withdraw further. Distancers usually react favorably to a loving, gentle approach. When they can proceed at their own pace, they feel safer about getting close, but when approached too vehemently or too frequently they get frightened and pull away. They can become so intent on warding you off that they can't tell whether they might enjoy being closer.

Be sure to acknowledge any efforts made toward being close. Remember, they are harder for your mate than for you.

If your mate is an intimacy saboteur or doesn't give you enough space Recognize that your mate needs more from you and try to compromise. Usually, instead of trying to control you, your partner merely needs approval and assurance of your love. With that reassurance, more independence and distance can be tolerated. Explain, in a nonrejecting way, that you need time to yourself. Help your partner to understand your feelings and your fears.

Try to understand what causes you to withdraw. Share your apprehensions with your mate, so that you can support and reassure each other. Describe ways in which your mate can make it easier for you to get closer. When do you feel more open to close contact and when do you need to be alone? Some couples devise signals to communicate when they are available or unavailable.

Learn to minimize negative interactions.

Examine your own possible contributions to your difficulties. You may be inadvertently encouraging the treatment you're receiving from your partner. By playing out the same role with your mate as you did with your parents, you may be fostering the very behavior you dislike. Don't encourage your partner to treat you as your parents did by behaving as you did when you were a child.

If, for example, you act helpless and dependent, you encourage your mate to take charge of responsibilities and decision making. If you want your mate to treat you more equally, you will have to change your behavior. By becoming more assertive and independent, you give reassurance that you can be depended upon. It then becomes easier for your mate to share the responsibilities of your relationship and household.

On the other hand, you may feel overburdened by obligations. In that case, it helps to examine your own tendencies to take control or to criticize others. You may be unwittingly fostering a situation in which you take care of everything.

Anne's father was very passive and withdrawn. Her mother was the strong one in the family, handling all the money, the running of the house, and the discipline of the children. Anne thus saw her father as inadequate. The man she married was quiet and easygoing like her father, but also very capable. Nevertheless, because Anne had internalized a view of men as inadequate, she saw her husband as unable to handle anything. Although she resented it, she took over many of their joint responsibilities, later getting angry with her husband for not doing enough. Without realizing it, she was creating the very situation she didn't want.

While you can't change your mate's personality, by interacting differently you can often change the nature of your relationship.

WHAT IF YOU ARE STILL DISSATISFIED AND UNHAPPY?

How to Deal With Your Anger

There is a widespread view that it is important for your physical and mental health to get anger "out of your system." But there is a great deal of current research, described by social psychologist Carol Tavris in her recent book, *Anger—The Misunderstood Emotion*, that contradicts this view. And common observation shows that merely expressing anger, without getting the response you want from your mate (or perhaps getting a negative response) doesn't make you feel better. In fact, it can make you feel a lot worse. The only time open anger is cathartic is when it achieves a positive result. If it is expressed against someone who allows it and responds by either fixing the problem or being appropriately sorry, you feel better. If your partner responds, as most partners do, by becoming angry and defensive or by withdrawing from you, you are likely to feel worse.

Sometimes, however, blowing up at your partner does achieve what you want. Threats and outbursts serve to intimidate your partner into complying with your requests. You may justify your anger by telling yourself that the other won't listen when you talk, and that yelling is the only way for you to get your point across. But, although you may be right, the results don't usually lead to greater intimacy.

There is no evidence that the mere physical discharge of anger makes you feel better. In fact, studies of children or adults who were encouraged to punch a pillow or scream for the purpose of physically discharging their anger show that it caused them to be more rather than less aggressive.

Talking to others about your feeling isn't enough to make you feel better, either, according to the latest research. Unless this talking leads to a resolution of the problem or to greater understanding, you are merely rehearsing the anger and increasing its intensity. Most discussions with friends and family about your grievances don't lead to solutions that get at the source of the anger. They merely make you feel justified at being more and more enraged at your partner.

On the other hand, keeping your feelings to yourself and doing nothing about them, or taking them out on your mate, yourself, or others because you don't understand the source of your anger, is equally destructive.

What does work? First, you must try to determine what is making you angry. Is there any contribution from your moods or other stresses this week or this month? Sometimes if you are having a bad day, week, or year, you are less tolerant of your partner.

Try to let go of trivial conflicts and fight only for the important ones. Sometimes the best thing you can do is let the issue drop and allow your feelings to dissipate. Other times, you should give yourself time to figure out if the issue is worth the struggle.

When you determine what you want to discuss with your mate, try to have a calm discussion. (Follow the procedures outlined in Chapter 14 for resolving conflicts through better communication.) Learn the difference between acknowledging or reporting your anger and acting it out. You can assert yourself and say how you really feel without insulting, accusing, or hitting your mate. When your level of anger gets too high and you are losing your sense of perspective—disengage immediately from the argument. You can't come to any satisfactory solutions when either of you is enraged.

The best way to dissipate your anger, according to the latest research, is to learn to see the situation differently. If you can understand the reasons for your mate's behavior and not take it personally, you will often feel less angry.

Of course, there are always times when anger is justified—when no amount of discussion or understanding will help you accept the situation. At such times, you will have to try to change the way you and your mate relate.

Determine What You May be Contributing to the Problem

If discussions and understanding don't resolve your problem, and your partner still continues to behave in ways that make you angry, what can you do?

It is possible that your own insecurities and fears are preventing you from being satisfied with your partner, or, you may have some other part in making your relationship dysfunctional. Careful self-examination (and perhaps a rereading of selected sections of this book) can help you determine what, if anything, that part is. In either case, working on your own problems may help. For example, if you overreact to your mate's reasonable comments because of your fear of criticism or control, you will have to resolve your problem rather than expecting your mate to change. On the other hand, you can expect your mate to be considerate of your feelings and careful not to attack you where you are most vulnerable.

After becoming stronger yourself, you may find that your mate's flaws don't seem as terrible as they once appeared. You may decide that what you are getting from the relationship is much more important that what you are missing. If you decide you want to be together, even though your mate may not be perfect, you have to learn to accept the other person and communicate this acceptance. All too often I have seen people complain about their partners over and over again and yet never leave them. Because they continually communicate anger and disappointment, they make their partners feel inadequate. Their partners may give up in despair, believing these people can never be satisfied.

Try to Encourage Your Mate to Change

Throughout this book I have emphasized looking at your own behavior and taking the first step in initiating change. That is because you can't force your partner to improve—you can only work on yourself. You can modify the way you and your mate relate, however. By refusing to participate in destructive patterns and by attempting to communicate in a calm rational manner, you can make your relationship better. In addition, you will often elicit greater cooperation from a partner who sees your efforts at improvement.

Nevertheless, sometimes partners don't change. What do you do then? Let your partner know what you want in clear and simple terms. Then wait and see what response you get. Although at first your mate may react unfavorably, avoiding you or trying to control you even more, there may eventually be an effort to change, to keep from losing you. If your mate can't—or won't—change, then you will be in a stronger position to leave. If you have worked on your part of the problem, and your partner hasn't made any effort, you will be less likely to feel guilty if you decide to end the relationship.

If You Are Thinking of Leaving

What can you do if you feel you've done all you can to improve your relationship and are convinced that the problems are not due to your own fears, overdependencies, or unrealistic expectations?

Many clients ask me if they should leave their partners. I find this question a very difficult one to answer. However, when they ask me if they should try to work on their relationships or instead work toward leaving, I have no problem. Both these goals are reached by the same method. The qualities and strengths needed to succeed in an intimate relationship are the same ones it takes to be able to leave a bad one. If you work on your feelings of independence, self-esteem, and identity, you will be better able either to stay and make a success of your relationship or—if that isn't possible with this partner—to leave successfully.

First you must ascertain whether you are staying only because of your insecurities and fears. You may be afraid of change—you know what this person's like but you don't know who's out there. There is a strong pull to stay with what is familiar (that may explain your choice in the first place), which may be keeping you in a bad relationship.

Many of you fear you will never find someone else. Women, especially, read about the scarcity of marriageable men and feel that if they don't hold on to what they have, they will have nothing. You may be afraid to compete in the "meat market" of the singles' scene. You may be fearful of being alone or of not having enough money. Many today are fearful of dating because of AIDS.

Another common cause of remaining in a bad relationship is low self-esteem. If you see yourself as the major problem, you will keep trying to make the relationship work no matter what the cost. You will try harder, do more for your partner, and be more tolerant of flaws. You may feel that you have invested so much in this relationship that you can't give up now. To do so would be proof that you really aren't good enough to have a relationship. People who feel this way often believe that if their current relationship doesn't work, no other relationship will be successful either.

Usually these fears are unfounded. Just because one—or even more than one—relationship is unsuccessful doesn't mean that the next one won't work. Although there may be many IAs in the singles' scene, there are also many men and women who want closeness. In addition, as you can see from the previous descriptions, many IAs can change.

By understanding why you are staying in your unsatisfying alliance and trying to work on your fears and insecurities, you can often overcome them and take the risk of leaving.

If You Can't Do It Alone—Get Help

Changes are not easy; they require a great deal of adjustment on both sides. Sometimes you make the changes and your mate is unwilling or unable to adjust. Other times you are the one who finds it difficult to change. People with all good intentions who are trying very hard often cannot overcome some of the fears, bad feelings, difficulties in communications, or conflicts that prevent them from being intimate. They feel trapped in a situation that is not satisfying and yet are unable to leave it, which leaves them feeling anxious, depressed, or otherwise in distress. This is when they have to go for help.

If you determine that your relationship needs help, turn to a professional rather than friends or family. Although well-meaning and caring, friends or family generally fail to understand the real issues and can make matters worse. They cannot avoid taking sides. Although they may offer emotional support, they cannot help you resolve the conflicts between you and your partner. A real danger is that they might advise breaking up when that is not the answer.

Be careful, also, about confiding very personal and painful complaints to friends and relatives. You may get immediate relief because you feel understood, but such confidences tend to back-fire. While you wouldn't knowingly confide in anyone you didn't trust to understand or keep quiet, secrets are hard to keep and people somehow "slip" and reveal too much. And when you and your mate resolve your problems or make up, your confidantes will still remember your problems, which can be embarrassing for everyone concerned. They might carry grudges and stay angry with your mate for hurting you. Although you, loving your mate, may forgive and forget, they can't. Even if your confidantes don't stay angry, your mate may feel betrayed because they know such intimate details of your relationship.

16

When You Can't Do It Alone

WHEN IS PROFESSIONAL HELP NECESSARY?

When the Relationship Is in Trouble

If two people find they can't talk to one another and work out their problems together, it is sometimes useful to have a third, objective party help with communication. There may be tremendous anger and hurt preventing them from hearing each other, and they may or may not be fighting a great deal. (Sometimes they just withdraw emotionally rather than fight.) A therapist can help to diffuse the anger and teach them to communicate effectively. It is often easier to understand what your spouse is feeling when a therapist helps with the explanation. Also, the therapist can get below the surface to the real issues underlying the superficial complaints.

Sometimes problems between couples are deeper than difficulties in communication. There may be gaps in expectations that the couple cannot bridge by themselves. They may be locked in destructive interactions from which neither can escape. One or both of the partners may have already thought about separation, and in those cases, especially, before any irreversible steps are taken, professional help should be sought.

When One or Both Partners Are Severely Distressed

There are times when the relationship seems fine, but one or both of the partners are not happy. They may feel anxious, depressed, or both. Physical symptoms (psychosomatic) might indicate the presence of excessive stress, as might the constriction of activities. One of the partners may be avoiding sex, or not going out of the house or on vacation in order to prevent anxiety. One may feel unable to get ahead in a job because of feeling hampered by inability to handle the added stress.

Sometimes a clue that indicates difficulties in a marriage is a child who is having problems. If any member of the family is in chronic psychological distress or in severe distress even for a short time, psychological help is usually indicated.

If one of the partners is unhappy or in psychic distress, the relationship may or may not be the problem. Other sources may be unhappiness at work or with other relationships, past or present. Psychological help is indicated for that partner's sake and for the sake of the relationship because very often, individual problems adversely affect relationships.

When You Can't Form or Maintain Intimate Relationships

If you have great difficulty forming intimate relationships, or find that none of them seems to work out, you have to suspect underlying problems. Perhaps some of your fears are interfering with intimacy. Perhaps you have unrealistic expectations of others or of what relationships should offer you. Any of the difficulties described in this book can be serious enough to require professional help.

When people are in distress, they are more likely to seek professional help. However, sometimes the only distress they feel is loneliness, which they rationalize as not being their fault. They can't admit that they have anything to do with the problem or that they can do anything about it. It is usually very upsetting at first to think that your "bad luck" with mates has something to do with you, either because of your choice of mates or because of your behavior. Ultimately, however, facing up to this possibility can be very important, because then you can change either your choice or your behavior and thus change your "luck." In order to become aware of what you are doing and why you behave in this self-destructive manner, you may need professional help. Once in therapy you can also begin learning to change your behavior.

WHY DO MANY PEOPLE AVOID COUNSELING?

Even when it is clear that counseling would help a person or a relationship, many people still reject this avenue. Why? Often they say they are afraid of what others might say or think about them. But what is more important is what they think about themselves and about others who seek professional help.

Most of these people feel that if you see a mental health professional, you must be "crazy." They don't realize that most clients are reasonably normal people who are having difficulties in the areas of work or personal relationships.

You often hear people say that they should be strong enough to handle matters themselves. This is usually voiced by men, but some women also feel that it is an admission of weakness to go to a counselor. It seems self-indulgent to see someone specifically to talk about yourself. Yet these same people don't feel bad seeking help from an attorney, a doctor, or an accountant when necessary.

Another fear people have of seeing a therapist is that they will become dependent on the therapist—either for communication ("Can't we even talk to each other without a therapist?") or personal support. Good therapy encourages growth and learning, not dependence on the therapist. People who have this fear may actually wish for someone else to take care of everything, so that they don't have to.

Others fear that therapists or counselors will control them or tell them what to do. If this occurs, they have chosen the wrong therapists. The aim of both individual and couples therapy is to help people find out what they want and help them achieve it, not to make decisions for them.

People who don't understand what therapy does may also feel that they would be paying for friendship, that therapy doesn't do any good, or that therapists care only about money. To protect against any of these negative effects of poor and incompetent therapy, seek a qualified professional.

WHAT IS PROFESSIONAL HELP AND HOW DO YOU FIND IT?

Professional help is psychotherapy or counseling by a person who is trained and experienced in one of the mental health professions. When you seek professional help, it is important to choose carefully. Go to a well-trained and experienced person whose background is specifically related to couples and individuals with the types of problems that are encountered in intimate relationships. These professionals are equipped to handle the screening of deeper problems (what appears on the surface is not always the full story). They understand the dynamics underlying the superficial behavior. Well-trained therapists will diagnose your problems accurately and help you choose the type of therapy that is most appropriate to your situation. Less competent or inexperienced therapists, like well-intentioned friends, can sometimes cause problems and even precipitate separations that are not called for. They may get caught up with side issues and not recognize the real issues, side too much with one person, or be unable to defuse temporary anger.

When deciding on a therapist or counselor, you should also look for someone who you feel is not judgmental or trying to impose personal values. Counselors should be supportive when necessary but not so much so that other perspectives are not offered. They should offer a protective environment, but encourage growth and self-examination. For example, a counselor who sees only your side and never points out your contribution to the problem or your partner's possible viewpoint does you a disservice. You may feel better talking to that counselor, but you will not learn anything about yourself.

Mental Health Professionals

Before you choose, you should know the different types of mental health professionals and their various psychological orientations.

Clinical Psychologists   Clinical psychologists have a Ph.D. in psychology, which includes a minimum of one year of clinical internship and additional practical experience. They study normal behavior, abnormal behavior, learning, perception, motivation, and other areas of psychology. Their training encompasses academic psychology, experimental psychology, and the understanding and treatment of psychopathology. In addition, in order to be licensed to practice in most states they need two years' postdoctoral experience and must pass an examination. Many clinical psychologists have additional postdoctoral training in a specialty.

Psychiatrists   Psychiatrists are M.D.s who do their three-year residency training in the specialty of psychiatry—the study and treatment of psychopathology—during which they study drug treatment, electroconvulsive (shock) therapy, and psychotherapy. In their pre-residency training, they study general medicine. Many psychiatrists also have post-residency training in a specialty.

Clinical Social Workers   Graduate social workers have an M.S.W., which represents about two years of graduate study including practical training. Clinical social workers place special emphasis on working with people who have problems. Some get advanced training in psychotherapy.

Marriage Counselors   Marriage counselors should have training in psychiatry, psychology, or social work before they are trained as marriage counselors. Someone who is trained only as a marriage counselor or a sex therapist will not be trained enough to treat any but the most superficial situations. They may refer you to someone else if your problem is more than superficial.

Sex Therapists   Sex therapists may be members of any of the mental health professions (or not) who then receive additional training that generally focuses on a behavioral approach to specific sexual problems. If there are other, deeper problems within your marriage or with one of you, sex therapists will usually refer you to someone else.

Types of Orientation

Behavioral The behavioral orientation emphasizes changing behavior without concerning itself with causes. Behaviorists emphasize only what they can observe directly. They work on symptoms or specific behaviors that the person wants to change. The methods used are reward and punishment, learning by imitation (role playing and modeling), and desensitization (exposure to fearful situations in graduated steps so that fears gradually diminish).

Cognitive behaviorists believe that it is what we tell ourselves (our thoughts) that determine how we feel and therefore how we act. By identifying irrational beliefs and assumptions and showing how they determine behavior, they hope to influence people to change their behavior. Cognitive behaviorists don't concern themselves with the reasons for irrational thoughts.

Family Systems The Family Systems approach views the couple or the family as a complex interaction in its own right, distinct from the individuals. The therapist pays attention to the balance of power, the particular alliances, and other factors. They see the problems in families as due to faulty interactions of the members rather than to intrapsychic problems of the individuals.

Psychoanalytic The psychoanalytic orientation emphasizes understanding the problems of the individual and couple in terms of both their conscious and unconscious thoughts and feelings. It deals with present behavior and the past sources of this behavior. According to the psychoanalytic school, in order to feel and act differently, you need to understand how and why you feel as you do. Most therapists who do psychoanalytically oriented psychotherapy do not analyze everything about the person, merely the things that are causing the problems.

Eclectic The eclectic orientation consists of some integration of the above approaches. The therapist may have a basic orientation and integrate other concepts and techniques where they might be useful.

Individual Therapy Versus Couples or Family Therapy

When is couples or family therapy indicated? Couples therapy can be very helpful in dealing with problems in communication between couples, in helping to assess the underlying dynamics of the interactions, and in setting up positive patterns in interactions. It is useful in dealing with power struggles and miscommunications, and in helping parents build a relationship with and separate from their children.

Family therapy is effective in assessing family dynamics: the interactions and interrelations of family members, shifting alliances, and the balance of power. Family therapy can often help the less involved parent become more involved with the children, and it can offer the weaker members support in dealing with the others.

When is individual therapy indicated? Very often the couple's difficulties can best be treated by one or both of the members' receiving individual therapy. Many problems—usually deeper internal problems—are best dealt with individually. Unreasonable needs and expectations or problems with giving or trust fall into this category. Their resolution is sometimes not merely a matter of better communication or of compromise.

When is a combination of therapies indicated? When the problems in a relationship can be worked out through greater communication and understanding of the dynamics, couple sessions are helpful. Very often, however, there are also individual problems that need to be dealt with separately. Sometimes it is a "secret" that one of the members has (an affair or secret feelings, perhaps). Or sometimes one or both of the partners are not sure that they wish to remain in the relationship. More often it is a matter of individual problems, which are best dealt with individually. In those cases, a combination of therapies is indicated.

Afterword

While this book is written about Intimacy Avoiders, the emphasis is not on the extreme Distancer or the person who can't relate. Most of the people described in this book are not pathological—not emotionally disturbed or sick. They are like you and me, trying to get the most out of life and relationships. But they are hampered by fears or insecurities.

Most of us avoid intimacy to some degree. There are times in our lives when other needs or goals conflict with our need for close emotional contact. When we are building a career or when our children are very young, it is easy to become sidetracked and lose sight of the importance of our relationships. Most couples don't recognize the early signs of this. They don't notice until an uncomfortable distance has developed between them. Then they can't comprehend how their relationships suddenly became boring and unsatisfying. I hope this book will help these people identify the specific problems that are interfering with their closeness and emotional satisfaction.

By recognizing the particular patterns of behavior that you and your partner may be using to avoid intimacy, and by seeing how others changed these patterns and improved their relationships, you can learn to improve yours. But reading this book is not enough. You need to put its principles and suggestions to work.

Most of us don't expend enough energy on relationships. We don't expect success at work to be effortless—we train for our careers, work hard, and do what we feel "has to be done" in order to get ahead. However, we don't like to think of relationships as requiring work. We prefer to believe that they will take care of themselves.

Intimacy requires effort. It requires removing the veils that separate us from our mates. It requires understanding our own vulnerabilities and working on them so that they don't interfere with closeness. It also requires reaching out to our partners, trying to understand them, and communicating with them.

I hope this book will help you and your mate to accomplish this and achieve greater intimacy in your relationships.